that ministry takes. There are inspiring and challenging questions, as well as practical insights. Not just useful, but a trigger for reflection on my own call and ministry as priest.'

The Revd Dr Sandra Millar, Head of Projects and Development for The Archbishops' Council

'Jonathon Ross-McNairn and Sonia Barron have drawn together a rich and diverse range of perspectives on what it is to be a curate in today's Church. Honest about the joys, challenges and sometimes difficulties of being a curate, the book highlights telling insights and important questions for all those involved in the curacy process. As such, it will make a valuable contribution to the thinking and practice of all those concerned to see curates flourish in the early years of ordained ministry.'

The Revd Canon Dr Andrew Braddock, Director of the Department of Mission and Ministry, Diocese of Gloucester

BEING A CURATE

Stories of what it's really like

Edited by
Jonathon Ross-McNairn
and
Sonia Barron

First published in Great Britain in 2014

Society for Promoting Christian Knowledge
36 Causton Street
London SW1P 4ST
www.spckpublishing.co.uk

British Library Cataloguing-in-Publication Data
A catalogue record for this book is available from the British Library

ISBN 978–0–281–07096–1
eBook ISBN 978–0–281–07097–8

Typeset by Graphicraft Limited, Hong Kong
First printed in Great Britain by Ashford Colour Press
Subsequently digitally printed in Great Britain

eBook by Graphicraft Limited, Hong Kong

Produced on paper from sustainable forests

This book is dedicated to all ordained men and women who have said 'yes' to God's call to serve him.

Contents

Contents

Acknowledgements

—————◆•◆•◆—————

The editors are grateful for the support of many colleagues and friends who have helped give birth (as one contributor put it) to this book, especially to Trevor Cooling, Howard Worsley and John Witcombe for talking us through the process and giving us some very good advice at the outset. Particular thanks also to Graham Tomlin, who encouraged us to take the book idea forward.

We thank all our contributors who willingly gave their time to write up their experiences to share with others, and all those who have generously given their time to read scripts and endorse the book.

Our special thanks are due to Alison Barr, our commissioning editor, for her insightful advice when reviewing the scripts; and of course to her editorial team at SPCK.

Finally, we thank our spouses Emma and Tom, who have graciously allowed us time away from family and other commitments to work on the project. Without their support, encouragement and input it is highly likely that this book would not have been completed.

Foreword

Every few weeks, as a bishop, it's my privilege to license people to new ministries. Almost always the service will include a solemn moment when the licence and authority for ministry is read and handed by the bishop to the new incumbent. The bishop says: 'Receive this cure of souls which is both yours and mine.'

The word 'curate' comes from that phrase 'cure of souls' and it describes something very important at the heart of ordained ministry. Sometimes the words are paraphrased as 'the care of God's people', but they mean much more than this. A deacon or priest is called to help people to know God in Jesus Christ, and through Jesus to find healing and salvation in their lives. People live in families and communities, and the cure of souls involves ministry in the name of Christ to those families and communities as well as to individuals. The cure of souls which is entrusted to a new minister at a licensing service is far more than the pastoral care of the congregation. It is a responsibility and concern for the wellbeing, healing and salvation of everyone who lives in the parish, inside and outside the Anglican congregation. As the words imply, the cure of souls is a shared ministry: shared with the bishop, with fellow clergy, with authorized lay ministers and with the whole people of God.

A curate is someone who is learning to share in the cure of souls, normally alongside one or more experienced priests. A curacy is a time for learning and growing, when you feel the weight of the ministry entrusted to you but don't yet have to bear the full load.

God calls all kinds of people to ordained ministry and, as part of their ordained ministry, to be curates: old and young, rich and poor, men and women, from every class, race and social background. Everyone's experience of the journey to ordination and in their curacy is different. It really helps to listen to other people's stories and insights.

This book is a rich resource of personal stories and insights about serving as a curate. They will help you to understand the different parts of the journey and what this ministry is like today. As you read it, especially if you are exploring the path of ordained ministry, remember God's grace and love and remember God's call to a lifetime of ordained ministry in all kinds of roles with, at the centre, the cure of souls.

Steven Croft, Bishop of Sheffield

Introduction

This book is a collection of personal stories and reflections about being a curate in the Church of England. There are contributions from a broad range of people who are either curates themselves or who are or have been involved in curacies in some way. The book as a whole, through a blend of story and reflection, seeks to answer a number of key questions, including 'What is it really like being a Church of England curate?' and 'What can we learn from the stories and reflections of others who are involved in the curacy process?'

It is intended for anyone who finds themselves at some stage in the curacy journey – whether already a curate, about to be ordained, in training or making those first steps of discernment towards a possible vocation to the priesthood. It is also intended for those who have responsibility for the training or oversight of curates or who may simply be curious about the reality of ordained life in the Church of England – thus the subtitle of the book, 'Stories of what it's really like'. Whoever you are, we hope that you will find something in this book that will inform and perhaps even inspire you.

The book starts with a look at ordination training from an ordinand's and a training principal's perspective. We have not considered selection and discernment as there are plenty of resources available in that area. We then move on to consider the pre-ordination retreat, the ordination service itself and those first few days in the strange new world that is ordained ministry. The Bishop of Gloucester, Michael Perham, takes us adeptly through these stages. There follow a number of contributions from curates or recent ex-curates, all telling the story of their curacy experience.

In our brief to contributors we emphasized the importance of contributions being real and grounded in order to offer an honest reflection about being a curate and curacies. Each story is, of course, different and can only be a 'snapshot', but taken together we hope that they will give you an insight into the reality of being a curate in the Church of England. Where necessary, the names of individuals mentioned have been changed in order to ensure anonymity; where names have not been changed, the prior consent of those concerned has been obtained.

You will notice that at the beginning of each chapter there is a profile of the author. Our intention is that the contents of this book should be representative of the breadth and depth of the Church of England, and so there are contributions from men and women in differing contexts and from different church traditions. Recognizing that while all books have their limitations, we wanted our book to be as broad and inclusive as possible.

One of the key questions in relation to curacies is 'What makes a good curate and a successful curacy?' We have included a number of contributions that specifically address this question. As Lincoln Harvey points out in his chapter, the key relationship in any curacy is that between the training incumbent and the curate. We have therefore included two chapters written by experienced training incumbents looking at the nature of this relationship. There follows a chapter by Rosalyn Murphy on making the transition from curate to incumbent. There is no doubt that this transition is significant and needs to be carefully prepared for. While a single chapter can scarcely do justice to such an important topic, we have included it in order to highlight some of the areas to think about when moving on at the end of the curacy.

Unfortunately, some curacies encounter difficulties, despite the best of intentions. As Howard Worsley points out in his chapter, 'You do not have to travel far in the Church of England to find a story about a difficult curacy.' No book about being a curate would be complete without facing such a reality. This chapter – helpfully we hope – includes some thoughts and advice on how to address 'thorny issues' when they arise and also how to personally survive a difficult curacy.

We finish the book with a brief reflection on the value of sharing stories and some practical advice drawn from the contributions in this book and our own curacy experiences.

We are extremely grateful to all our contributors. It is an obvious point to make, but this book would simply not exist without their time, effort, prayer and thought. They have shared their stories and reflections with great insight, honesty, humour, warmth and generosity. It is not always easy to share our experiences, and some of the stories in this book do not make for easy reading. But it is important that the breadth of curacy experience is represented and that you, the reader, should be able to glimpse what it is really like *Being a Curate*.

Jonathon Ross-McNairn and Sonia Barron

Part 1
ORDINATION TRAINING

1

An ordinand's story

JONATHON ROSS-McNAIRN

Jonathon is a full-time stipendiary curate. Prior to ordination, he practised as a commercial property solicitor in London and also served in the Army as a commissioned infantry officer. He trained for ordination at St Mellitus College in London and was ordained in Gloucester Cathedral in 2011. His church experience is predominantly in the evangelical tradition but his curacy is in an Anglo-Catholic setting serving two churches in Gloucester, one urban and the other rural.

* * *

There were quite a few people who had thought it strange that I should train to be a vicar. Part of me agreed with them. It did feel a bit odd but nevertheless I was able to start ordination training full of confidence and assurance. There were a number of reasons for this.

First, I was a recent 'Alpha convert' having come to faith through a powerful conversion experience on an Alpha course. I had encountered the risen Christ in an 'imaginative vision', not exactly on the road to Damascus – actually in a hall on a Pontins holiday camp – but the experience was categorical for me. Second, my sense of calling to ordination had been clear and at times almost audible. I remember cycling home from work along Islington High Street almost hearing God inviting me to give up being a solicitor and offer myself for ordination. Third, I had raced through the formal selection process. The Church of England had given me a resounding 'yes' and had publicly validated my vocation to the priesthood. So on day one of training I was keen and raring to go. It was undoubtedly a high point in my journey to ordination. However, my sense of confidence and assurance was not to last long.

As the training got under way and I started to read theology in depth, I found myself having to examine some of the assumptions underlying my faith. For example, I knew that Jesus had died on the cross for me, but what did that statement actually mean when examined? In addition, I had to grapple with penetrating and difficult questions. For example, how could a supposedly loving God allow so much suffering in the world? I call these 'supermarket' or 'bus stop' questions, because I have found as a curate (and an ordinand) that these are the places where people often ask such questions. It pays to have thought through some sort of an answer. I remember one particular evening in the pub with friends during my first year of training. They had asked me some fairly predictable questions and I had felt woefully inadequate in how I had answered them.

Over the course of the first year there was an emerging and uneasy sense that my faith and theology were being deconstructed and it all felt rather uncomfortable. I was entering a place of unknowing and uncertainty. The situation was also not helped by the fact that I – at least initially – simply could not understand much of the theology I was reading. It just didn't make sense to me. There was a new theological language and a way of thinking to be learnt.

About halfway through the course, my father was diagnosed with terminal cancer and was given only a few months to live. My college work, particularly the essays, were metaphorically speaking thrown into the corner and I put my energy into caring for him. But if I had thought for a moment that I could put my theological training on hold or to one side I was certainly mistaken. Now I was faced with some very hard and intensely personal questions. Should I speak to my father about faith and salvation? If so, how and when could I do this? And did I have anything coherent or helpful to say? I was now not only in a place of unknowing but in a place of vulnerability, confusion and fear. My two 'worlds' of 'theological training' and 'real life' were colliding and I was standing in the middle. I spent quite a bit of time simply not knowing what to do or say beyond the practicalities of everyday life and looking after my father.

But I had to do and say something. After all, I was a vicar in training and my father's life was coming to an end. I could have called in a local priest but somehow that didn't seem the right thing to do. I had to step up to the plate. And so I sat with my father and held his hand while he died. I stood by his bed in the early hours of one morning and gave him the last rites. I didn't know what I was doing. I had simply looked up the relevant section in *Common Worship: Pastoral Services* and said the prayers for him. He could not speak at this stage because he was so unwell, but he could squeeze my hand to indicate he had heard me. It is one of the hardest things I have ever done and also an immense, almost indescribable privilege. As a curate there will be times when we will feel completely out of our depth, but if we are able to respond to whatever the situation is, in the best way we can, then my experience is that God will honour our efforts.

After my father died, I found myself at rock bottom. I was in grief and at a real low point in my life and journey towards ordination. I was significantly behind with my college work and 'my theology', once neat, tidy and assured post-Alpha, was now in what seemed to be an irreconcilable mess and muddle. There were also the practicalities of the funeral to sort out and a eulogy to be written and delivered. Disturbingly – but perhaps not surprisingly – people also turned to me for guidance, prayer and answers. I managed somehow to keep going in coping mode, but internally I was struggling. There was a real conflict between how I was presenting in public and my interior life. I was in a place of vulnerability and inadequacy and I felt deconstructed. My reflection is that I was in fact at the cross and I struggled to accept this.

Without doubt, it was God who led me from the cross to new life. The first thing that I needed to realize was that God had not abandoned me but was and had been fully present despite the awfulness of the situation. The key turning point theologically for me was being introduced to Carmelite spirituality, which had a profound effect on my relationship with God. I explored the works of John of the Cross and was particularly struck by his analogy of 'the dark night of the soul'. The analogy is that we may encounter times when it seems that God is absent, but in fact he is so close that we are blinded by his light. As I reflected on the experience of my father's death, I came to realize deep within myself that I had in fact never been so close to God. It was as though he had been walking very closely beside me. I learned then an important lesson – much of ministry is about noticing God at work even in the mess and muddle of life. He *is* there despite how we may feel. Sometimes we just need to look a little harder. Where is God when someone we are with is dying? Perhaps he is in the hand of the one who holds the hand of the dying person because that is an expression of love and God is love.

Having assured me of his presence despite the circumstances of life, God encouraged and at times gently cajoled me towards a new way of being in relation to others. I noticed that I began to open up to the people I was training with, and that they listened. I learned a new language of prayer grounded in honesty and rawness. I was the prodigal son on my knees in a state of poverty and vulnerability. I began to accept some of my limitations and weaknesses. This was not without a struggle but it was also liberating. I came to realize that God was not calling me to be perfect but that he calls each of us as we are, with all of our gifts, oddities and failings. We are work in progress!

I also started to connect with God through different forms of worship and formed real friendships that continue to this day. I began to see the importance of being resourceful and reaching out for help when

I needed it. This is vital as a curate. There will be times when we feel that we simply cannot cope. My advice is to form and sustain prayerful friendships with people you can trust and rely on. You will need them.

I also discovered – and perhaps I was a bit slow on the uptake – that training and formation properly happens in community. The importance of this cannot be overstated. Ordination training should not be a solitary exercise or a body of knowledge to learn or a set of skills which we seek to acquire. It is much more complex and demanding than that. The training experience at its best should encourage and enable the giving of the whole self into a supportive, prayerful learning community so that we can discover something deeper about ourselves and about God.

My reflection is that this is something that I needed to learn about ordination training because it contrasted sharply with my previous experience of professional training. When I had trained to be a solicitor, I had studied for the exams and in time had become a competent practitioner, but I had intentionally held back something of who I was. There was the Jonathon who was a lawyer and the private Jonathon who had a life outside work. Ordination calls us to live integrated lives, where the whole person is offered in the service of Christ and his Church.

By God's grace, and by properly being and learning in community, I began to change – slowly – and to be formed into the person God was calling me to be. It was undoubtedly a disturbing and surprising process because I had to face up to who I really was – the good parts and the not so good parts. I particularly valued the group work in this respect. Sometimes we do need to offer a little more of ourselves than we might feel comfortable with, and trust that those we are with will prayerfully honour and support our efforts to express something of who and where we are. My advice is not to hold back but instead to take the opportunity during training to explore feelings with others, because those others can often help us to see situations in a new light.

I began to 'reconstruct' and my theology began to (re)form. I began to make new theological connections, sometimes in surprising places. For example, I remember finally understanding (or at least thinking I understood – there may well be a difference) Luther's theology of justification by faith, on the tube near Paddington. A strange experience, but it also felt exciting because – at least to me – it meant that I was making some progress with my understanding of things theological.

The beginnings of answers to some of those big questions also started to emerge. In this respect, my learning was greatly enabled by interacting with my fellow ordinands and tutors. We would share stories, encourage each other, laugh together, eat and drink together, pray together and try to work out what on earth the latest essay question meant *together*. I remember many a late-night conversation in the college bar where I would end up in a sort of theological cul-de-sac, but sometimes I would be able to make some progress in my thinking and understanding. As ordination approached, I was growing in confidence and assurance. I sensed that I was on an upward curve to a new, better place, a new high point, but it was a different sort of assurance, this time with theological depth and a broadening of my spirituality and worship experience. I had done more than survive ordination training. I had grown and changed, and I enjoyed the sense of being 'reconstructed' again. This is not to say that I approached ordination with all of the answers and in a state of 'holy perfection'. Far from it! But my journey had been truly formational.

As the end of the course came, I started to recognize the trajectory I had been on – an unexpected and challenging journey from 'life' (a high point) to 'death' (a low point) and then to 'new life' (a new high point). My story in this way resonates with Christ's own journey to the awfulness and vulnerability of the cross and then to new life through the resurrection. My reflection is that sometimes our experiences during training – in the curacy, in life – will take us to the cross whether we like it or not. I did not want to be in that deconstructed place of uncertainty and struggle, but there I was. Being at the cross will mean different things for each of us. Our calling is not to avoid it but to accept it in the confident hope and expectation that God *is there too* and will, if we allow him, lead us beyond the cross towards new risen life.

It would be comforting to be able to write that with my training experience behind me the curacy experience was comparatively plain sailing. Not at all! There were many more challenges and ups and downs to come. My advice, for ordination training and for the curacy, is to expect the unexpected. It *is* a journey and sometimes things happen on that journey which we do not expect and do not want to happen. But – vitally – *God is there.*

Being ordained is a wonderful privilege but at the same time it can be incredibly demanding. You will need to look after yourself – physically, emotionally and spiritually. Explore how best to do this during your training. But perhaps above all, realize that we cannot do ministry in our own strength and must therefore live by the words in the Ordinal: 'You cannot bear the weight of this calling in your own strength, but only by the grace and power of God . . . Pray earnestly for the gift of the Holy Spirit.' This is probably the most important lesson for ministry and one that I continually need to be reminded of. And one more thing, if I may – learn to pray as you can and not as you can't. For me, I pray best while I am out for a run around the parish.

2

A training principal's reflection

MIKE PARSONS

———◆•◆•◆———

Mike has been priest-in-charge of a council estate parish in Gloucester since late 2011, before which he was Principal of the West of England Ministerial Training Course (WEMTC), a Diocesan Director of Ordinands (DDO) and Director of Curate Training, a team rector in a multi-faith inner-city area, a research fellow in a theology department and a curate in north London. Before ordination he was an academic physicist and once belonged to the research group that achieved the world low-temperature record. He continues to have an active research interest in the relationship between science and theology.

* * *

When I had finished my own three-year residential course at a theological college, gaining a degree in theology and spending a lot of time playing cricket (which was not part of the curriculum), the very last thing on my mind or in my expectations of where God might lead me was teaching in a theological college. By that stage I had been in a university setting as student or teacher for 13 years, and I wanted out. It just shows you the truth of the rather corny saying that if you want to hear God laugh, tell him your plans!

Which illustrates one of the tasks for theological colleges: how to prepare ordinands for a ministry that may not even exist at present and how to help them be open to discerning where God might lead them next. Stipendiary ministry in the Church of England involves a commitment to deployability; in principle you could serve in any diocese. Ordinands train either for self-supporting ministry (SSM) or for stipendiary ministry. Many SSMs move to stipendiary posts after a first curacy: some change to stipendiary ministry during training. In all cases you may be asked to serve in a parish you might not choose to worship in as a lay person. As a stipendiary minister this is almost a certainty at some point. We all need to face this and ask if we (and our families) can cope.

The Church that does not yet exist

At WEMTC, we were always very conscious that we were preparing students for ministry in a Church that does not yet exist. Culture, society and people's expectations have changed hugely over the last 30 years. Increasing prosperity has driven up wages and pension expectations and the Church cannot possibly afford the staffing levels of the 1980s, let alone the 1950s, even if the personnel were available. Yet so often congregations (and sometimes clergy) dream of a past golden age when all was wonderful. This age, which is in any case largely illusory, will never return and we have to learn to proclaim afresh the gospel to the current generation. Clergy in training will serve for 20 or 30 years (or even longer) and we need to give them tools they can use in the future to interpret society, rather than solutions that have proved effective for today's situation – which may be quite inappropriate in 20 years' time. There were, I believe, two important emphases that helped towards achieving this aim. The first I inherited as part of the existing WEMTC theological ethos; the second was a result of having to extend my own theological education into areas unknown when I was in training.

Theological reflection

Theological reflection was the first area – and probably the more important. I never cease to be amazed when curates, usually from the traditional residential colleges, groan, 'Not this again – we did it to death in college,' when it comes up in the post-ordination training programme. This usually means they don't understand it and don't practise it either! An unreflective priest is never going to lead a flock to meet new opportunities. Terry moved from a south London suburb to the north-east as a team vicar. Early in his ministry he came home one day after some baptism visits and said to his wife, 'I need to rethink everything I thought I knew about baptism. This isn't working here.' Clergy are not alone in needing this discipline – becoming a reflective practitioner is now a normal part of the continuing professional development programme in most professions.

There are many methods of theological reflection, but like many things it is important to teach one tool well rather than many superficially. In WEMTC we taught a technique we called the Theological Learning Cycle (see Figure 1, overleaf). It is the same process described by Laurie Green in *Let's Do Theology* and it is the very first thing that everyone does. It is well known but often poorly applied: proceeding from Experience to Action *via* Exploration and Reflection.

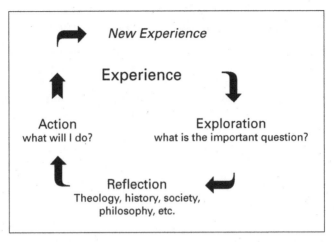

Figure 1

As its name suggests, it is a cycle. First, perhaps, an experience hits you. For example, you are really upset because, led by one or two dominant members, there has been a big row on the PCC about the noise children make in church. The temptation is to jump straight to the action phase – which could be anything from 'keep the children out of church' to telling the objectors that 'Jesus loves the children so they'll have to put up with it', and everything in between. What you have *not* done is identified exactly what question you want answered, so you are unlikely to have resolved the issue in any significant way.

Margot was a very senior nurse manager and was quite sceptical of this method when it was introduced in her first week or so of training. At the end of the first term she shared with us all that it had been an eye-opener:

> I've had no end of management courses where [this method] was used, but you always knew there was a 'right' answer the management expected you to come up with. For the first time I've seen how it can lead me to a quite new course of action. I'm going to use it this way at work now.

This process of reflection was used so often and in so many different contexts that it became second nature. It rubbed off on the staff as well. We had a difficult term when a student and his young son were killed in a car accident, another student's husband died suddenly at work and a youth worker known to many took her own life. I took the memorial service for the youth worker and found myself using the cycle to ask,

'What is an appropriate pastoral response to suicide?' Out of this grew a Grove Booklet, *Suicide and the Church: A Pastoral Theology*, as well as a significant number of pastoral conversations with students and others who had experienced the suicide of a friend or relative and had never had the opportunity before to explore their feelings.

Teaching doctrine through missiology

This was the second main emphasis of our work at WEMTC. Julian, an ordinand and a teacher at a local boarding school, commented to me that he appreciated the teaching and its applicability to daily life. 'If it didn't work in the staff room or the classroom tomorrow, I'd be back to let you know,' he volunteered (or possibly threatened!). This made me reflect on the importance of mission in the way we approached ministerial formation, and was very timely since I was in the process of revising a major advanced doctrine module. *Mission-Shaped Church* had recently been published and the question of exactly what was the Mission of God (*Missio Dei*) for the Church in the twenty-first century occupied my mind. The approach we adopted was to teach doctrine (in other words, what we believe and why) through missiology rather than as a set of given topics handed down from on high. Missiology didn't seem to exist when I did my training (maybe it was something 'they' thought you only needed if you were going to be a missionary). It is the study of how and why the Church has grown, how it has understood its purpose over the centuries and what motivates it. It comes as something of a shock to many to discover that this has been very different in different periods of the Church's history. But it is so important for a Church where tomorrow is not going to be the same as today, let alone yesterday.

A simple example of teaching the doctrine of the Trinity is given by Lesslie Newbigin, and arises out of his experience in India evangelizing animist tribes. The first task was to tell them about Jesus, God's Son, our Saviour. Very soon, however, they would ask if this Jesus was God, or a lesser god, or one of many gods. So as you answered them you discovered why the early Church spent so long talking about just how Jesus could be God and Man, and the relation between the Father and the Son. Then, in so many cases, you would discover that in various ways God had already been working with this tribe; so you discovered in your experience the work of the Holy Spirit. The Trinity had emerged from your missiological experience.

The Church needs to understand how the context it finds itself in affects how she answers the most important questions of our faith, such as:

1 Who is Jesus?
2 What is the Church and how do we experience it?
3 What of the future – when will God reign fully?
4 What does it mean to be saved?
5 What is it to be human? Are we fallen and corrupt – or on our way to a greater unfolding?
6 Is culture good or bad, irrelevant or a vehicle for communicating the gospel?

So began for me, and I hope for many others, an exciting journey of discovery, to work out how these fundamental questions, asked by humankind through the ages, might be answered in today's society.

In doing this we used film and video clips quite a lot: the world often asks questions in a profound way and if we want to contribute to the answers we need to hear the questions being asked. Several students commented ruefully that their families complained that they could watch nothing at home now without the danger of a theological reflection making an appearance! One staff member's daughter became adept at pointing out to Mum films and other resources that she could use in teaching. You would be surprised how much mileage there is in *Kung Fu Panda* concerning personal identity, or in *Dead Man Walking* about forgiveness and redemption, or in *Fight Club* about understanding people in their twenties and thirties. We are here to tell the story of what God has done through Jesus: use any means possible!

The training context

Whether they are full time or part time, a really important part of the training comes from students interacting with each other – particularly in the bar, which is often the only communal area available. Discussions can get very deep and sometimes touch on sensitive and painful areas of students' lives. In residential training these things generally happen in the college context, in common rooms and private rooms. For non-residential students they happen during weekly evening lectures and weekend residential courses, often in places adapted from other purposes.

One of WEMTC's highlights were 'the residentials' in a Methodist hotel, where the food was superb but there was no bar. Our Methodist students were at the forefront of solving this problem by the conversion of an external living block into a bar, which was named in their honour – the Wesley Arms. It even had its own pub sign and, what is more, was legal as one student had a personal licence to sell alcohol. Some accommodation was much less luxurious, however, and two of the places we used suffered a fire after we had left (no connection, we hope). A local Catholic convent was used quite a lot: it has wonderfully welcoming nuns, little idea of heating in the winter (bring your thermals) and a brilliant pub right opposite that didn't seem to know what closing time meant. The nuns even saw the funny side of being woken up at 3 a.m. by two students who couldn't remember (or were incapable of remembering) the code to get back in. The local pub not only provides a place for relaxing and group bonding: discovering that a bunch of apprentice vicars had turned up led to interesting group discussions on more than one occasion.

Facing doubts

It is very common in training to feel that you are questioning beliefs and practices you have held to be fundamental, an essential part of your spirituality. This is normal and is not an indication that you are spiritually slipping or failing in any way. Listen and learn from the experience of others. I discovered that students found it particularly helpful when I told them of how I had lost my faith for a short time while in training. My studies had led me to a point when I thought I had explained everything away. I didn't want to upset people, or disturb their faith: it was near the end of term and I would have a quiet word with the principal and just say a few goodbyes and go. For a day after deciding this I experienced huge peace. I was calmer and more together than for ages. I was sitting in my room, reviewing exactly what I would say and why when I came to a sudden halt. I became aware of what I can only describe as a presence in the room. My reaction was, I'm afraid, 'You b—, you're still here!' That experience has been important to me for over 30 years now.

Not all students, I'm afraid, are able to confront their doubts. Bruce put them all to one side and became very hard-line about certain matters, yet inside he knew the questions were valid. I fear a breakdown at some point in the future. Gareth, however, was fascinated by the claims of Islam and was intellectually capable of studying it deeply. But to do so honestly he had to negotiate a break from pastoral placements, as to engage with integrity with another religion meant he had to leave open the possibility that the Christian position he held was wrong. He now teaches and advises on Islam with a faith all the stronger and gives leadership to the Church in many areas.

If God has led you this far he can be trusted with your doubts and uncertainties, but you have to give them to him rather than pretend they are not there. It is often more a case of faith growing into a deeper, stronger and more mature form, but with fewer supports. Questioning can be dramatic or quiet and hidden. I remember a student on a residential course leaving the chapel, clearly distressed, during a Eucharist. Both I and the other member of staff present were glad to see two other women follow her out to help, holding a box of tissues – and returning saying 'We need more tissues.' Ministry will as often come from the other students as from staff and we saw a lot of this in the difficult period we had with several deaths. These supportive relationships have been carried by students into their later ministry and deeply valued by them.

Ministry calling?

Ken worked as an aircraft mechanic and in the aftermath of September 11, 2001 found the staff on the airfield where he worked in shock and looking to him, their resident Christian, for some way of expressing their bereavement and solidarity with those who had died and their families. A short memorial service he led in one of the main hangars was attended by many and added to his call to ordination.

For many students, the crises they experience are not about their faith, but are much more mundane; yet they may be equally pressing. How on earth can I write essays at my age? How do I balance home, church and study? Do not fear, you will be offered help with study skills: and often assessments are based on project work or collaborative enterprises. At many colleges and on all non-residential courses, exams are a thing of the past. We were also very clear with students about priorities: family must come first, followed by your job, then your studying – and involvement in your local church has to be the last, possibly along with some much-loved leisure activities that you may not have time for while in training. There are sacrifices to be made.

Eileen has a wonderful singing voice which she formerly used at a semi-professional level. But she could see that there would not be time to pursue both her singing career and her ordination studies. She laid the singing to one side, which was a great sacrifice and one she agonized over. Ministry can be costly.

Ordinands come from a range of backgrounds, and part of the formation process involves a parish placement that opens them up to new experiences, sometimes with dramatic results. The non-residential courses draw students from all backgrounds and churchmanships and a notable part of the experience is how they learn from each other. Sally had come from a Baptist background and a very informal, community-based evangelical local church. Placing her in one of the diocese's largest – and definitely Anglo-Catholic – churches was going to extend her, but she was up for it. The staff prepared her with careful briefing and support, but she came back bubbling over with enthusiasm for what she had discovered: a whole new dimension to her spirituality. While remaining an evangelical she is now ministering in an Anglo-Catholic parish, where she is building a fresh expression on a housing estate.

On one occasion our more Anglo-Catholic students complained we never had a really Anglo-Catholic Eucharist with all the trimmings. So we did, and I had to learn to swing a thurible (the metal pot on a chain with the burning incense in it). I'd never done this before in my life, but there were a couple of willing instructors and I practised outside the chapel censing a pair of mobility scooters. I mastered figure-of-eights and 360s: I was proud of my achievement. And I now know who put the video of my efforts on YouTube: I'll get my own back!

Residential or non-residential?

Ordinands usually have a choice between residential and non-residential training, though for some family and employment circumstances make only one option easily achievable. Nowadays half of all ordinands and a great majority of female ordinands will train on non-residential courses. Do such courses provide a second-class training, with residential training as the gold standard? There have always been some who believe this, but the evidence suggests otherwise.

I did some research during a sabbatical on the formational experience of a representative section of those ordained over the last ten years, with equal numbers for the residential and non-residential modes of training. What was not surprising was that those who had been residentially trained believed they had received a slightly more rigorous academic grounding than their non-residential colleagues. What was initially a surprise was a clear indication that those who had attended non-residential courses believed that they had much better training in preaching and missiology. But they are grounded in a parish and local mission and have three years' preaching practice and reflection, as opposed to the two undertaken by residential students. They do contextual training by default and without consciously thinking about it, much as a fish probably doesn't think too much about water!

All those who responded to the survey were very positive and buoyant about their training, which was good to hear. The only group who felt less than enthusiastic were those who attended a residential college but had to commute some distance daily or stay over a few nights a week. They lost out on the residential experience because they often weren't there. They would, however, have got much more experience of living in community on a non-residential course: six weekends a year and an eight-day summer or Easter school. There the residential experience is concentrated and intense.

When making the choice about where to train, you will get a lot of advice from other clergy, your vicar, the DDO and even the bishop. Some speak from real experience and have important advice, but remember, it is a long time since most of them trained and their favourite college probably has changed a lot since they were there. By far the best way to approach this decision is to visit two or three colleges and courses (there is only likely to be one non-residential course possible for you) and talk to the students. See which one you (and your family) like.

Be prepared to change

If you are about to start training, try to see it as a time for change and development. I often ask candidates in interviews for various posts to reflect on how they have changed over the past five years. This process of change is growth and it needs to be there all our lives, whatever we do.

Staff as well as students experience change, and for me, one of the joys of theological education is seeing ordinands develop and grow while realizing that I am growing and developing as well. I have been deeply affected by the pain our women students have felt when confronted with a Church that sees them as a problem, and I am aware that at times I might be part of the problem. I have come to realize that while temperamentally I prefer to be something of a 'lone ranger', actually I need others, and I need to be present at communal events as part of this little section of the body of Christ. It is very humbling at the annual oils service on Maundy Thursday in the cathedral (when the bishop likes all his clergy to be present) to look round and see just how many are there because I have had the privilege of playing a part in their journey to that point.

Regional courses were only just being thought about when I was in training, but by the time I was a DDO they were established all over England. Being principal of one of these courses has been a joy and a privilege, accompanying men and women on what is for many an arduous and sacrificial journey of training, transformation and growth. You become a support, a mentor and friend to women like Jenny, who left school with almost no qualifications, dispatched with the condescending message to 'go and get a secretarial job, dear', as she struggled to understand how this call to ministry in later life could possibly make sense. It was tremendous to share in her joy as she discovered that it was dyslexia that had been holding her back and to see her first get her foundation degree and then take on the option of the top-up course to get her honours BA.

I think I am remembered for a number of things by past students: repeated name-dropping, encyclopedic knowledge of Scotch whisky, the ability to get science and religion into most topics, likewise 'postmodern' and 'paradigm' . . . and, spectacularly, the advice in one particular end-of-term game (which entailed passing the baby down the line without hands) of 'just get your boobs under it, woman!' But most of all, I hope, I'm remembered for the repeated conclusion in so many classes and sermons, that all we are called to do is to tell the story and share the glory.

Part 2

ORDINATION AND FIRST STEPS

3

Michael Perham

—•◆•—

Michael Perham has been Bishop of Gloucester since 2004; he is due to retire in November 2014. Before becoming a bishop, he was a curate, bishop's chaplain, parish priest, cathedral precentor and dean. In all these ministries he has worked with ordinands and curates. A writer in the areas of theology, liturgy and spirituality, and one of the architects of the Church of England's Common Worship, *he has espoused passionately the cause of the ordination of women to all three orders of the Church. He is also Chair of the Governors of Ripon College, Cuddesdon and Bishop Protector of the Franciscans.*

* * *

Wednesday lunchtime

For this bishop, and for others like me, the three or four days running up to an ordination are some of the most important, and indeed the most encouraging, in the year. I guard these days from those who want to put other things in my diary during that period, for this is to be time with the ordinands. Of course, every bishop and every diocese approaches these days in a slightly different way and I can only describe what has worked for me (and I think for my ordinands) over the last nine years in the Diocese of Gloucester. But I am happy to do so, partly to encourage ordinands, but also to encourage fellow bishops to throw themselves into these pre-ordination days as times of grace and growth for themselves as well as for those whom they are going to ordain.

For me it all begins on a Wednesday lunchtime, when I pray for sunshine, before 10 or 12 potential deacons arrive on my doorstep, accompanied by spouses or partners and sometimes babes in arms and toddlers wanting to get out of buggies. They will be joined by much the same number of deacons soon to be priested and by members of my staff team. There could be 50 or more of us for lunch. It's my chance to welcome the candidates and their families and to launch them through good hospitality into some significant days. Because I am not the 'sponsoring bishop' in the diocese – the suffragan bishop does that – I've sometimes not met some of the deacon candidates before, and very likely not their families, so it is an important time to establish relationships. Not all the ordinands will know one other. Those who have been at college or on the local training course together are feeling fairly secure. They are with their friends. But some ordinands are the only one present from their particular college and course. This is an important moment in beginning to integrate them into the diocesan family and into 'the class of two thousand and whatever'.

After lunch there are rehearsals in the cathedral so all shall go well when the ordination day comes. Suddenly it all feels very real indeed as the candidates find themselves standing before the bishop, rehearsing promises and practising kneeling for quite a long time. They probably enjoy the sight of the bishop and the cathedral precentor metaphorically dancing around one another, each trying to be in charge of the rehearsal!

Then come the Declaration and Oaths. Some candidates seem more prepared for this than others. This is the moment when ordinands are to declare their understanding of the Church of England, its history, its heritage and its doctrine and promise to lead worship only in the forms allowed by canon law, to give allegiance to the sovereign and to promise canonical obedience to the bishop 'in all things lawful and honest'. I sometimes think I ought to talk through at that point what exactly they are signing up to, but perhaps it is a bit late by then; the hope is that it has been covered during training. Certainly for me the oath of canonical obedience is important in establishing a relationship between me and these new clergy, and establishing the obligations between us that we all need to take seriously.

In Gloucester, tea follows at the Deanery, with the dean playing host and the members of the chapter present. We want the ordinands to understand from day one that the cathedral in which they are soon to be ordained is a place where they will always be welcome, one which might sometimes feed their soul. But, just for now, it's also about feeding them with strawberries, cake and iced coffee. After that, the ordinands take leave of their families. Next time the spouses greet each other, one of them will be a deacon. They both wonder what difference they will make. The candidates (and the bishop) go to Evensong in the cathedral. Even those for whom cathedral music is a strange new world seem to find it a helpful calming experience. But, once it is over, it's into cars (with some sharing) and off to the retreat.

Wednesday night till Sunday

For the next three days, there is the opportunity to leave behind all busyness, to enjoy quiet, reflection and a rich pattern of worship, to have some significant conversations, but above all to find space and sleep. There to help is the retreat conductor, a priest who can bring wisdom, insight, humour and a bit of theology through a series of addresses and through personal conversations. At this stage ordinands don't need either academic theology or pastoral tips. They just need to be drawn closer to God. That's what I ask of someone if I invite them to lead the retreat.

For me worship is at the heart of the retreat. Many years ago, when I was a dean, I asked a group of ordinands on the day of their ordination, when they had returned from their retreat, how it had been. 'Wonderful addresses,' one of them said, 'but the worship was all over the place.' Worship that's all over the place doesn't help, and next year I found myself as the retreat conductor and I worked hard to put together a Retreat Worship Book. Every year since then it has gone through a number of revisions, to refresh it and to reflect the retreat conductor's themes, but it remains at the heart of our retreats.

Within it, alongside the Eucharist, the office and *lectio divina*, are three liturgies particular to preparation for ordination. Each needs to come at the right moment over the three days and, in my experience and that of my ordinands, they are deeply affecting moments. On the first full day of the retreat is a Liturgy of Healing and Reconciliation, a chance to let go of past hurts and failures. It includes the laying on of hands, anointing and silent prayer by all who gather in the chapel. On the second day there is a Liturgy of Foot-washing. The Ordinal permits the bishop to wash the feet of the new deacons in the ordination service itself. I have never felt entirely comfortable with it in that setting – it is not a spectator liturgical act! For me the setting of the retreat is the right one, and in that situation I delight to get down on my knees and wash the ordinands' feet. That too, I believe, helps shape the relationship between bishop and deacon. On the third day, we gather before lunch for midday prayer, the renewal of baptismal vows and the ordination charge. The Renewal of Vows, with each person coming to the font and dipping his or her hands into the water, always feels like the right last act before the Ordination, a reminder that the calling of a new deacon or a new priest is always an extension of the more fundamental calling through baptism to be a disciple and minister of Christ.

The ordination charge is my final word to the ordinands before we go to the cathedral. Traditionally the bishop doesn't preach at the ordination; often the retreat conductor does. So this is my opportunity to talk to the ordinands privately but collectively and to say the things that I most want them to hear as they begin their new ministry. I regard it as a rather solemn moment. It's a serious charge, not just a jolly chat. It's written down and I email it to the newly ordained the following week. Just occasionally, clergy remind me long afterwards of what I said, which means that they have taken it as seriously as I do. Of course, it builds on the individual interviews I have had with candidates during the retreat, during which I unfailingly hear profoundly moving stories of the journey of each to ordination. Often these involve the overcoming of immense challenges – of which the first is often wanting the call to ordination to go away, but finally accepting and embracing it.

A retreat is, for some ordinands, a new experience; for others it has long been part of their spiritual discipline. An ordination retreat needs to take all that into account, which is part of why we usually have a degree of compromise between silence and conversation. In Gloucester, it's normally silence from after supper till before lunch each day, including silent breakfast, but conversation at lunch and supper and during the afternoon. Some would like more silence – they can always creep away to find it. But bonding, which is also part of these days together, requires some conversation. And, if silence is imposed for too long, nervous laughter is liable to break out, most likely in the middle of a silent meal. Of course, there is also conversation with those back home and, in order to allow for a modicum of that, but not too much, we encourage the ordinands to turn off their mobile phones, except for a pre-arranged time when they are going to talk to their family. Some are really grateful for such a rule (and for being able to blame the bishop for it!); others find it a real challenge.

Certain sorts of conversations within the retreat are, of course, important. The retreat, even at this eleventh hour, can bring out issues that need talking through. Just occasionally, though not often, there is a real crisis – 'Can I go ahead with this?' Sometimes the Director of Ordinands is the person to whom the anxious ordinand talks, sometimes the bishop, sometimes the retreat conductor. Sometimes ordinands choose, within the retreat, to make use of sacramental confession, even if it is not ordinarily part of their tradition, and then it is usually to the retreat conductor that they go for such ministry.

In Gloucester, Saturday afternoon sees the deacon candidates going to the cathedral and sitting as a group to watch as the new priests are ordained. If not friends already, they will have become so during the retreat. They return to the retreat full of excitement, wanting to unpack the event and relate it to what is to happen the next day. It's the task of the retreat conductor to tune them back in to retreat mode, with a short address at night prayer before an early night.

Sunday

Next morning it's morning prayer before breakfast and then putting on the clerical shirts and the dog collars, with a certain amount of nervous amusement as the ordinands look at one another thus attired. And then to the cathedral for the event for which they have long waited. There gathered will be a vast congregation of their family, their friends (often a lot of unchurched ones among them) and future parishioners. No candidate would be able to doubt the huge support and affirmation for them there.

An ordination, like other sacramental acts, is placed within the Eucharist, so much is familiar – greeting, collect, readings, sermon, peace, eucharistic prayer and all that follows from that through to the dismissal. But within that context there are the special moments – early on the presentation of the candidates and later their interrogation by the bishop in a series of demanding questions, the consent of the congregation to their ordination, much prayer and then the laying on of hands by the bishop – which, with deacons, is done by the bishop alone; with priests it is the whole college of priests that shares in the laying on of hands. The new deacons wear their new stoles, over their right shoulder as a sign of being a deacon, either from the beginning of the service or from after the Ordination Prayer. They are given a Bible or New Testament as a sign of their authority to teach and preach. They begin to exercise their ministry as deacons – perhaps by 'laying the table' for the Eucharist, sharing in the distribution and one of their number giving the dismissal with which the liturgy ends. The chances are that their exit with the bishop through the cathedral, all joy and smiles, will be met with thunderous applause. Then, of course, comes the photoshoot!

It's a big service. You cannot avoid the fact that it will be quite long, for there is a lot to include, though people remain engaged as it moves through its many phases. And there are so many people. Yet in the middle of it all there is a strange intimacy. Ten or a dozen men and women gathered in a semi-circle around their bishop as he presides at their ordination, he and they close enough to see the powerful effect of the words and actions on each other, close enough for them to sense his encouragement and his confidence in them, close enough for him to see both their nervousness and their joy. 'Send down the Holy Spirit on your servant *N* for the office and work of a deacon in your Church.' It is an awesome and genuinely Spirit-filled moment.

Monday and Tuesday

Some days will elapse before the bishop sees the new deacons again. The ordination over, they are reunited with family – there is excitement and pride, sometimes surprise on the part of less churchy family and friends who have been bowled over by the service. There's almost certainly a parish or family party. And then there is sleep – it has been an emotional day. And Monday morning? A wise training incumbent will not expect too much. Mine, nearly 40 years ago, took me to a pub for lunch on Monday. But by Tuesday it was time to inhabit this new role. Nowadays there will be a working agreement to help shape that new ministry – so there will be no great surprises about the structure of the day, the pattern of weekday worship, the expectations about meetings with the incumbent or the choice of day off. Almost certainly there will be key people in the parish to visit. There may even be a first funeral, at least to attend and assist, put straight away into the diary.

But there will be all sorts of other surprises, most of them good ones. There will be surprise that relationships with people one has known before change. There will be surprise that the collar opens doors and facilitates unexpected conversations. There will be joy at finding gifts one didn't know one had. There will, of course, be also the beginning of the long search for balance between work and the rest of life, though that is not a challenge restricted to clergy. There will be the need to work at the new key relationship with one's training incumbent. If that relationship is good, it is the very best foundation for ministry in all the years to come. It is worth working at – on both sides.

If you are a Gloucester deacon you are, however, back with the bishop within a few days, to spend a bit of time looking at something very specific – the liturgical role of the deacon, not just for its own sake, but because it is intended to model what the deacon's ministry is intended to be in terms of service, support and proclamation of the gospel of Jesus Christ. For me, meeting with the deacons, a few days on, enables me to do some teaching about that, warning them that at some stage in their first year they will find themselves as the deacon standing at my side at a diocesan service, and that I want them to inhabit that role confidently. It also enables me to talk to them about the diocese in which they are now serving as deacons; how I want them to belong, to have a sense of collegiality with all the clergy of the diocese, and how those who work for the diocese centrally, the bishop included, are there for them.

In the retreat and in the ordination, relationships will have formed. For me it is an enormous privilege to share the retreat with the ordinands, to hear their stories and then to lay hands upon them to ordain them as deacons and probably later as priests. I always want to build on that time together so that we can go on nurturing one another's ministry among the people of God.

Part 3

STORIES OF BEING
A CURATE

4

Lincoln Harvey

———•◆•———

Lincoln is an associate priest at St Andrew's, Fulham Fields, having first served his curacy at St John-at-Hackney in east London. Prior to ordination, Lincoln worked in theological education for a number of years, teaching Christian doctrine in various institutions, before taking up a full-time post as lecturer in Systematic Theology at St Mellitus College where he continues to teach. He is the author of A Brief Theology of Sport *(SCM Press, 2014).*

* * *

Experts sometimes joke that three factors should determine whether to rent or buy a property: location, location, location. With curacies, however, things are a little different. The most important factor is your incumbent, incumbent, incumbent. I was extremely lucky with mine; others are far less fortunate. But location remains a big factor in any curacy, even for those of us who stay where we are and do not have to move anywhere. This is because ordination takes you to places you had never imagined. The familiar is transformed.

Once ordained, I was to continue in my work as a theological educator, diligently exploring the intellectual beauty of the gospel alongside ordinands in training, a delightful task. I was also to remain at St John-at-Hackney, my parish church, where I had been saying my prayers during the discernment process. I was delighted. I had lived in so many places during my life that a bit of stability was very much welcome. I was confident that familiarity would not breed contempt.

My final Sunday as a layperson arrived quite quickly. Fr Rob had decided to mark the occasion properly, and so – as the liturgy drew to a close – he called me forward out of the pews. Then, in a loud booming voice, with his arms outstretched, he pronounced God's blessing upon me and sent me on my way, propelling me out into the future through the stunned silence of the congregation. My departure from church did not go unnoticed. Everyone in the congregation knew I had left.

Two weeks later, my re-entry into church – as the newly ordained curate – was also marked, not least by the transformation in my clothing. Standing at the front of church, I was now equipped with a dog collar, cassock alb and a colourful stole. I definitely looked the part, even if I had little idea what I was doing.

The first few services whizzed by in a blur. I think I had been imagining that not much would change. I had envisaged the same old me, doing some new things, in some wonderful new clothes. But I was wrong. Ordination proved much stranger than that. It was a *different* me doing new things in peculiar clothes. I was now a changed man.

I had not undergone the fabled ontological change in quite the way imagined, had not been somehow mysteriously transformed into a new substance (the product of ecclesial alchemy, as it were). Instead, the change was much more relational: everyone was now treating me differently. For a start, they were calling me 'father', and demonstrating a certain respect and deference for my role through their body language and behaviour. But the greatest change was more subtle: the wonderful people of St John-at-Hackney were much *nearer*, somehow more immediate, vulnerable and open, present to me in a way that was radically new. I was now closer to the people, so to speak.

With hindsight, it felt as if I'd been *relocated*. I had been transported away from my old pew at the back of the church to a strange new seat in which I was somehow alongside everyone. All distances had collapsed: old, young, rich, poor, black, white, whoever, everyone welcomed me as *their* curate. The entire church was now my next-door neighbour. I had become *public*.

However, the transforming nature of ordination was not as positive as this description makes out. I came to realize that it had also changed me in a way I did not like: it had taken me away from the people, as well as moving me nearer to them. The distance became apparent at a funeral. Our church community had been stunned by an unimaginable tragedy, with the terrible loss of one of our most-loved children. The funeral was indescribably sad, the burial unimaginably painful, and the wake – held in church – extremely emotional. During the wake, I became aware of a commotion outside the church. Venturing out, I was met by the sight of a small crowd, their voices raised as a number of policemen tried to calm people down. I could immediately see that the police had set up a large tent in our churchyard, which was clearly part of their stop-and-search initiative to crack down on local crime. To make matters worse, they had decided to search some mourners. People were very angry, and rightly so.

Now, I've never liked the police, and I wasn't about to start. But before I could ask them what on earth they were doing, I became aware that the crowd were treating me in an unexpected way. They did not see me as some sort of man-of-the-people, joining them in a necessary struggle against the idiocy of the police. Instead, they were treating me as if

I was *with* the police, as if I was some sort of chaplain to the powers-that-be, somehow on the same side as the government's henchmen. As clergy, I was part of the establishment.

Coming from a working-class family, with little more to my name than a chequered past, I'd always slept safe in the knowledge that when society broke down, I would be on the right side of the divide, aligned with ordinary people against the forces of oppression. But things were now different. Ordination had made me identifiably Church of England, immediately redefining me as a pillar of the establishment.

Up until that point, I had always been able to keep the Church at a bit of a distance, sitting lightly to any aspect of its public identity. I could dodge any criticism of Anglicans, cultivating some kind of personal space in which I could be me and the Church could be the Church without confusing the two. But that comforting space had now collapsed. My identity coincided with the public institution. I realized that I *am* the Church of England in some people's eyes.

This alignment of institution and person is partly what it means to get ordained. We can deny it, but we can't escape it. Of course, there is much more that needs to be said about ordination. Public identity is more complex and multi-faceted than this sketch suggests, and I certainly wouldn't want to deny the way ordination takes you closer to the people; clergy are able to represent the community in all sorts of situations, often being a voice for the voiceless, an agitator for justice, and the centre of grassroots initiatives for the good. Ordination opens up possibilities few of us could predict. And it is always an honour to enter the holy land of people's joys and griefs, to baptize a child, to marry a couple, to hold the hand of the dying and to bury loved ones; the list of positives is endless. Ordination is a genuine privilege for which I give thanks.

But the fact remains: it is *privileged*. To be ordained in the Church of England is to become – in many people's eyes – part of the establishment. Some clergy, of course, feel at home among the great and the good. But for others, this part of the job comes as a bit of a shock. Yet it is unavoidable. The Church of England still has a civic role. Ordination involves oaths of allegiance, acts of remembrance, and becoming part of the complex world of local public life. Our paths will cross those of mayors, MPs and local dignitaries, and somehow we are associated with them all. I don't quite understand it, but the ontological change – in part – is political. This was something I had not expected. But I should have. The clergy stand for the whole parish. We can't pick and choose. We are dealing with tax collectors just as much as sinners.

My advice is to face this fact. Try not to wait until you're standing in the cathedral waiting to be ordained. Try not to wait until your first Remembrance Day service when you're about to march ahead of soldiers in front of the mayor. Instead, discuss it, pray about it and explore how you can discover the gospel through it, because there is little point in thinking we can sit lightly to all this, quietly going about our private ministry at arm's length from the Church. At some level – for better or worse – ordination is to become the Church of England to people, and that Church is still established, like it or not.

5

Rachel Wilson

Rachel is a self-supporting curate in the parish of St Edmund's, Dartford. In her secular work, she is a personal adviser at Chatham Jobcentre Plus and currently works in the parish two days a week. Prior to ordination, Rachel worked in both the voluntary and private sectors. She trained for ordination at the South East Institute for Theological Education (SEITE) and was ordained at Rochester Cathedral in September 2012. St Edmund's is in a broadly Anglo-Catholic tradition of worship and is a member of Inclusive Church. Rachel has cerebral palsy and is a wheelchair user. She has two teenage children.

* * *

It is probably neither sensible nor desirable to try and articulate what a 'typical curate' looks like but I am certain that most people hold some sort of model in their heads, however ill defined. My conviction on this matter comes from two sources. First, I know that when I first thought I heard the call to ordination, I couldn't reconcile my picture of 'me' with my picture of 'vicar'. They just didn't fit − at all. Second, I have seen a similar bewilderment play itself out on the faces of my parishioners and others with whom I have contact, the first time we meet; their models of 'curate' and 'me' are often a long way apart.

Let me explain. First, of course, I am a woman. Of itself, this is hardly revolutionary. The other thing which is true of me is that I use a wheelchair and my cerebral palsy means that walking, coordination, balance and good posture are not things that I have ever found it necessary (or even possible) to learn. All of these things taken together mean that I often need to negotiate all the unspoken 'but how do you . . .' questions which articulate themselves on people's faces in those first moments of any encounter, particularly when I am in my clerical collar.

In the midst of such encounters, I have come to realize that helping people understand how I work as a disabled minister is as much part of my calling as presiding at the Eucharist or baptizing babies. The incredulity that I see in people's faces the first time I meet them is not so different from my own reaction when I thought I heard a call to ordained ministry: 'I don't wish to appear difficult, Lord, but I can't walk, and while we're having a chat, I'm not great at talking either.' (I had a debilitating stammer at the time.) 'But apart from that, it's a great plan . . .'

So began my journey towards ordination, with the startling realization that my physical circumstances are not a mistake and that I am called to ordination because of my disability and not in spite of it; coming to that realization in myself continues to allow me to answer similar questions when I see them in other people. Since my disability is not an obstacle to be apologized for or overcome, but simply part of what makes me the person I am, it is less of an 'issue'.

It may be true that some people's image of God is challenged by having me as a curate, but it is also true that I have watched the vast majority of people move from a tendency to want to 'mother' me, to a position where I feel respected and valued as a member of the clergy. My disability means I have a gift for dropping things, and meetings and services early in my curacy were characterized by over-anxious watching and rushing to my aid at the slightest sign that I might need help. Now when I drop things, people just ignore it, and that's the way I like it! Gentle but firm refusal of help – or gracious acceptance, when that is appropriate – has helped everyone learn when help is and is not required. People are now much more likely to comment on how much they appreciate the way I preside at the Eucharist, where once they might have said, 'What a struggle it must be'; I regard the change as a triumph.

My ministry has uncoupled notions of physical and ministerial competence which are so often unthinkingly bound together. No one can do everything, and my presence makes that OK; I hope people see that doing what they can is truly more important than apologizing for what they can't do. New people have come forward to offer to read the lesson and to serve at the Eucharist. Of course, they might have done so anyway, but I sense that having a curate who clearly finds some things difficult, as we all do, has made others willing to make themselves vulnerable by offering to serve.

Church members are not the only people who have had to be helped to see how the curate functions. Ministry has inevitably brought me into contact with people who are not accustomed to seeing a priest who operates sitting down. On ringing a local cemetery recently to advise them that I would be the presiding minister at a funeral, I explained that I use a wheelchair. There was a long pause, followed by, 'Well, that might be a problem . . . we need to be mindful of health and safety.' My initial reaction was one of incredulous fury, but what I actually said was, 'It'll be fine. I'll come and see you and we'll have a chat about it.' When I visited them, I acknowledged their anxieties and answered their questions. The service was conducted smoothly and without incident and when I rang two weeks later to advise them I would be conducting another burial, they just said, 'Oh yes, Rachel, same arrangements as last time? No problem!' Of course, having to constantly reassure people can be wearing, but I have to acknowledge that people are afraid of what they don't understand; I can either help them, or make them feel more defensive. However many times I have to bite my lip, helping to put people at ease must be more productive than alienating them.

Conversely, as a new curate and particularly as a deacon, it is sometimes necessary to affect an air of confidence and even competence which may not feel real at all. Sitting in my first funeral visit with a bereaved family, what did I say when asked, 'How many funerals have you done?' I settled on 'One or two'! It seemed to me that the family would not be helped by me saying 'None', since they already felt lost themselves and in that moment I was the closest thing they had to security.

Whereas some adults have struggled with having a disabled minister, children seem to have no such difficulty. School assemblies are a particular delight, as are times when children come into church. My wheelchair has made an excellent impromptu 'stone' which a gaggle of six-year-olds had to try and 'roll away from the tomb'. The children loved trying (and failing) to move it. Lots of questions followed about Jesus, angels, 'How does it move?' and 'Why can't you walk?' – all good questions and excellent opportunities for ministry.

As a self-supporting minister, my calling explicitly straddles 'church' and 'world'. With hindsight I completely underestimated the amount of time and emotional energy that doing both my secular and ordained work would take. I am especially grateful to my children for their continued support; remembering the 'family' part of the equation is essential to prevent burnout, yet it can all too easily get swallowed up.

However, I truly believe that having a presence in both spheres of God's world gives me credibility with people who do not naturally 'speak God', as well as continuing to challenge me to find credible answers to those questions presented by the often harsh reality of people's lives.

I wish I had been prepared, though, for those times in my working week when I feel the 'pull' of the parish when I am at work, and occasionally vice versa; just as tiring as the amount of time it takes is the emotional energy that is required in order to keep those competing demands in manageable tension.

Whatever the challenges of ministry, as I reflect on my ordination I have never been more deeply content than I am now. Fundamentally, work is what I do but a priest is what I am; it's indelible. I have watched myself change from a person who couldn't see how ministry was possible into someone who thrives on it. Whoever you are, if you think you hear the call but can't see how it will work, be brave, say 'yes' and see what God does.

6

Steve Clarke

———— ◦•◦•◦ ————

Steve is the vicar of St Andrew's Church, Whitehall Park, London. Prior to this, he was a pioneer minister in the city of Gloucester and curate at Gloucester Cathedral. Before ordination, Steve worked as a lay minister for Trinity Church, a charismatic/evangelical church in the centre of Cheltenham. He trained at Trinity College, Bristol and was ordained in 2010. As a pioneer minister, one of Steve's main areas of responsibility was to lead the Fresh Expression in Gloucester (FEIG) community, which came into being through a previous pioneer. He was tasked with leading and developing this community and exploring new missional opportunities in the city.

* * *

All of us have a story; our lives are shaped by encounters, experiences, knowledge, joy, pain and more besides. Jesus calls us to bring our story and place it within his Big Story of love and redemption. When he calls those first fishermen, Peter and Andrew, he does it by saying that they are now going to be fishers of people. In that moment Jesus, it seems, sees who they are, where they've been and all that they are becoming and says to them, 'Follow me.' Jesus invites them to bring that story and place it within the reality of God that is unfolding right now, through him. I was very aware when beginning my curacy that my story had shaped me in a certain way, which I continue to be so grateful for. Much of my experience was in a contemporary, informal setting, both in church and during training at college, and in these environments you learn to 'fish' in a certain way, how to read the waters, where to throw the nets, what skills are needed. I'd got used to how to do things in a way that worked for those settings.

I remember my first ever experience of preaching at the cathedral, an 8 a.m. Book of Common Prayer service. Preaching, I thought, no problem, I've done this before. I expected it to go well, the only problem being that the preacher is also the server/verger for the service. I'd never done anything like that before and even though Neil, my training incumbent, had walked me through it and I'd covered my service book with underlining and pencilled in instructions, I still managed to get most things wrong. I walked up to the altar at the wrong time, stood up and sat down in the wrong place, handed plates, bowls and cups in the wrong order. Neil tried to guide me through the service with an elaborate code of finger pointing and waving and yet it was no good. I placed myself at the door to say goodbye to people, thinking, hoping that with the cathedral being so big no one would have seen my failed juggling act at the front – surely people would have been deep in meditative prayer? After shaking a few hands, someone took my hand, held on tight, leaned in and said very slowly, 'Don't they teach you anything at college these days?' OUCH! It kind of felt like throwing my net in the water and coming up with nothing.

My expectations have been challenged, too, within the pioneer work I do, even though I am more comfortable and accustomed to the informal setting within FEIG. I recall encouraging people to pray in groups together, assuming that a more open-ended 'say what you feel' style of prayer space would work. Yet people found this did not help them to connect with God or pray together. Over time we explored other creative ways to pray, by using words, simple responses and creative liturgies or prayer spaces. It's very easy to get used to certain ways of doing things, and, good as they are, they will not work in every context. I needed to lovingly listen to the community I found myself in and respond by creating space for people to encounter God. I take comfort from the disciples' experience of letting down nets and catching nothing. Maybe through failure and mistakes we learn to cast our net in a new way, throw out to new water, learning from Jesus as we go.

Pioneers, by definition, are 'sent ones'. From the beginning I was given a very open brief. Essentially I was to be based at the cathedral for support and a sense of rootedness in a community, my regular point of contact being morning prayer; from there I had freedom to 'go', to be sent out to see what God was already doing and get involved. This is a gift. It's not often you are given such an opportunity. At the same time it is daunting. I found my posture in those early days was one of listening to the community and culture in Gloucester and also to the existing FEIG community, which had been through many changes in the past 12 months. My guess is that most pioneers are activists by nature; I certainly am. I wanted to get things done and yet found that listening simply takes time. Two pieces of wisdom came to mind. The first was from my former boss, Mark, who told me not to overestimate what I could achieve in a year and not to underestimate what I could do in three to four years; the second from my friend Steve, a vicar in Nailsea who always advises new curates not to take on too much in the first six months, even though the temptation is great. Honestly this was hard. I'd get together with my fellow curates, who'd be talking about preparing sermons, doing loads of funerals and visits, youth and kids' work, and I'd think to myself, 'My week looks nothing like that.' My weeks were filled with prayer walking, meeting people for lunch and coffee, reflecting on what was next with FEIG and pushing possible doors where I saw new opportunities.

There were two experiences that really helped me have the freedom to be available to others. The first was the realization that it was very easy to get into a pattern of simply moving between the cathedral and my office each day. I found on some days that I was 'busy' at my desk with administration, emails and other tasks. Why? This isn't really a desk job, after all. So I gave myself permission to be out and about, even if it simply meant doing some of those desk things in a public place like a coffee shop. The creativity and energy of being around others really helped and I got to meet people as well. The second experience was walking my then three-year-old son home from playgroup one day. We were walking down the main road into town, a fairly straight, normal road by all accounts, and yet one that in his eyes was full of hidden opportunity. He was swinging under bars, skipping up steps, running down slopes. What to me was simply a straight line from A to B, to him was a playground. I joined in, and though it took us a lot longer to get to where we were going it was a lot more fun. I felt God spoke to me in that moment and it was as if he wanted me to see life as a 'Holy Playground' – that under the Spirit's guidance the ordinary and everyday can become a new opportunity. It may take longer but it's more fun.

At FEIG we have been inspired to see the cathedral too as a Holy Playground. We realized that many of the gathering and prayer spaces we created in this amazing building were fruitful places of connection for us and those who were part of our wider network and so we simply embraced this more, seeking to establish a gathered church community, while embracing the space in a creative and diverse way, one example being a communion service that used different spaces in the building and different works of art that were in place for an exhibition.

I've adopted this attitude in other areas of ministry too, spending time looking for new opportunities to emerge out of the day to day. In many ways these aren't spectacular and yet the sense of 'Immanuel' (God with us) has been amazing, so they have all been very special kingdom moments. One of the keys has been the time and availability being a curate has given me, which I may not have otherwise had. One Saturday afternoon I was taking my son to the park and I bumped into Greg. Greg had been at our last FEIG social gathering in the cathedral, invited by a friend of mine who DJs at these parties from time to time. We exchanged the usual 'Hi, how's it going?' greetings, and then he paused before telling me how it was the three-year anniversary of his mum's death and he had been praying to her, asking for a sign. I resisted the urge to judge or even seek qualification on this statement or his journey. Instead I pulled out my phone and said, 'Do you fancy a coffee?' (We both really like coffee.)

What unfolded from that chance meeting was a weekly get-together, where much of the time I listened to his story, what had brought him to Gloucester and where he felt life was going. We soon became firm friends and I felt more and more able to join in the conversation. So much of what Greg spoke about and articulated, his longings and hopes for the future, chimed with Jesus' invitation to those early disciples, and it wasn't hard to include stories Jesus told or the ways Jesus related the kingdom of God to the everyday. One day Greg mentioned another friend asking similar questions, and so I asked if he thought there would be others who'd be open to joining in. Within a few days Greg called to say he had gathered a few people, and we chose to meet over lunch once a week in my home.

This informal group has continued for much of my curacy. We've had to adapt our arrangements as people have got jobs, moved and got married, but we've continued to meet, open up the Bible and pray together, relating it all to our daily lives. One of the joys has been seeing the guys begin to offer to host and cook food when we've gathered. These friendships, centred around exploring a relationship with Jesus, have been one of the highlights of my curacy, and they've come from the discipline of being available and open. I've discovered that being available is not passive but active, and doesn't happen from an office so much as putting myself in the way of what God might be doing. This has taken me to pubs, cafés, art spaces and music collectives. Not all of these opportunities have developed in the same way, but I've come to a place where I'm OK with that.

If I could draw together my curacy in one word it would be 'patience'. Paul speaks of patience when he talks about the fruit of the Spirit in Galatians, and elsewhere he says that love is patient. I have certainly had to allow God to grow the fruit of patience in me and have come to realize (mostly from getting it wrong) what loving patience begins to look like. It seems that people's lives take time to grow and develop and often don't fit into our timetables and expectations. I have sometimes needed the wisdom of close friends and mentors, both to see where and when I needed to lay down my own agenda and choose to take up loving patience, and also to see where the kingdom was developing, even if it wasn't how I had imagined it. I've realized that it takes courage (which I have sometimes lacked) to step out and lay down self-centred expectations. There is much room for me to trust the direction and rhythms of God's Spirit, as I seek to be guided by him. Let the games continue!

7

Lusa Nsenga-Ngoy

———————

Lusa is the vicar of St Aidan's Church, Gravesend. Prior to ordination, he worked as a religious studies teacher in Brussels and a researcher in African development. He also worked as pastor of the French Protestant Church in Canterbury. He trained for ordination at Cranmer Hall, Durham and was ordained in 2008. His church experience is in the evangelical tradition, but he served his curacy in a liberal Anglo-Catholic setting in a rural church in Canterbury Diocese. He is currently a member of the Bishop of Rochester's Formation and Ministry team and chair of the Vocation Strategy Group for Ministry Division and the Committee for Minority Ethnic Anglican Concerns.

* * *

A Francophone, black African-born and Belgian-educated curate in a Kentish rural parish? What could go wrong? This chapter is an exploration of the particular experience of a non-Briton called to minister in a quintessentially British institution. Besides, it is an invitation to re-evaluate our definition of what it means to be an Anglican minister in a changing and polarized society. Ultimately, it is a call to assess ministry from a place of hurt and vulnerability.

I was sitting in an internet café in Pretoria when I first read of Staplehurst as a possible destination for my curacy. To celebrate my thirtieth birthday, I had decided to treat myself to a six-week South African holiday. This was a welcome break following six years of ministry with the French Protestant Church in Canterbury, before heading to Cranmer Hall, Durham for further training.

Returning to Kent after a year in Durham was an exciting prospect. Besides, it would finally give me a chance to get to know this little place whose name I had only heard as one of the stations en route to London. 'Staplehurst. This is Staplehurst.'

My first experience of this place and its people left me with a sense of warmth and congeniality. Little did I suspect that the following four years would have a dramatic impact on my life. No sooner had I arrived in Staplehurst, than I was already packing my bags to spend a remarkable three weeks in Canterbury for the Lambeth Conference. I was privileged to be asked to act as the deacon for the introductory Eucharist and help during the conference as a rapporteur. I recall a number of conversations with friends who suggested that it would be downhill from there. Looking back, it seems to me that those three weeks were only the start of a period of profound transformation in my understanding of ministry and myself.

The experience of the Lambeth Conference was the best possible introduction into ministry in the Anglican Church. Many came to the conference dreading a nasty and bitter confrontation. But most left with the strong sense that in a world where differences often spark hatred and division, the Church can commit itself to rise to the challenge of unity and offer an alternative way of living out differences through beautiful disagreement, having made progress in terms of mutual understanding and trust. The debates were not always smooth, as they contended with diversity in culture, context and psyche. Though they did not all reach a common understanding, and will probably share diverging views for a long time, there was something potent and inspirational in witnessing bishops wrestling together with difficult and polarizing issues in respect, selflessness and love.

I keep in mind the image of two bishops, one from the USA and the other from Tanzania, whose context and theology had become polarized. They had agreed to go on a walk on the attractive site of the conference, each trying to convince the other of the validity of his own argument on matters of human sexuality. After a long walk, their conversation came to an impasse as the path they had been walking on literally came to a dead end, while they had both failed to bring the other to embrace their views. The American bishop then turned to his African colleague and asked, 'What do we do now?' The Tanzanian bishop simply replied, 'We carry on walking.' Many have since carried on walking side by side, endeavouring not so much to persuade others of the validity of their argument, but to value and honour each other's integrity.

I left the Lambeth Conference with the sense that ministry is not always about consensus, but a call to create a permissive space for a variety of voices and opinions to hear one another. The rifts may never be bridged, theologies may not change, but hearts can be transformed and new relationships established. Is this not what our gospel is also about?

I returned to Staplehurst with a deep sense that ministry is, after all, not about arriving, but journeying. The curacy was to be the beginning of an ongoing process. I had no doubt that the way ahead would be paved with many joys and challenges. However, I moved forward with the knowledge that it need not be a solitary journey, but one that could be shared with many, each bringing his or her own theological, cultural and spiritual specificity in this wonderful mosaic that our Church is called to become.

What was it that I was bringing to the mix? As a young, black, African man with a continental education, it is fair to say that I did not necessarily fit the mould of what a conventional curate looked like at All Saints, Staplehurst. In fairness, all of my predecessors and contemporaries offered specific gifts and characteristics that helped to enrich our shared ministry.

I remember walking around the village, trying to get acquainted with my new surroundings and being struck by the fact that there were hardly any black faces around. That took me back to my initial experience of landing in Brussels as an eight-year-old boy from the Congo and finding myself, for the first time in my life, part of a minority group. Being 'the only black in the village' caused me to want to engage anew with my eight-year-old self and explore the often painful process of integration and adjustment to new environments.

For most of my time at school I was often the only black child in the class, and certainly one of just a handful of black pupils in a school of more than 800 students. I remember having the impression that, every time Africa was the focus of a lesson, my colleagues were seeing me for the first time. It was as if they had forgotten that I was the same boy with whom they had discussed the previous evening's film on TV, argued about the weekend football results, or passionately debated politics and religion. I now blame their reaction on the degrading and often inaccurate way in which teachers spoke about Africa and Africans. The experience taught me to explore further my own roots and develop a convincing apologetic of my people and my land. Furthermore, it left me with the challenge of integration without compromising myself. It made me able to culturally navigate both my world and the one I was called to inhabit.

Being black in a sea of whiteness is not always an easy experience. It is, at times, a balancing act, one that takes practice, especially when ethnicity becomes the main frame through which one is spoken to or about. On a good day, it was always nice to meet people in the village and not have to constantly explain who I was because the whole village knew that 'we' had a black curate. It was great not being part of the unending stream of invisible people. It is always good to be seen. However, on those rare days when I suffered from a deficit of grace, the umpteenth comment that they 'could understand every word of my sermon' was often met with an internalized, 'Well, what did you expect? That wasn't Kiluba [my mother tongue].'

Although it felt at times that I had been Photoshopped into this idyllic corner of Kent, I knew that my presence in Staplehurst was of God's doing. It is not so much that the place needed me, but that

I needed to be in that place at that time of my journey of faith and my journey in life.

As I progressed in my curacy, I became increasingly aware of the correlation between integrity in ministry and integrity with myself. There was no way I could effectively minister to the people of the parish if I was not prepared to share the whole of me in the process. If God has called the whole of our person into ministry, it implies that we cannot leave aspects of who we are out of the practice of ministry. Equally, it means that aspects of who we are can define the way people receive our ministry.

'For you,' said Augustine to his congregation at Hippo, 'I am a bishop, but with you, I am a Christian ...' As we enter into ministry, we might appropriately aspire to a life in which the self is subjected to a higher calling, a higher sense of being. But whatever and whoever we are will inevitably be drawn into ministry.

I came to that painful realization when, one day, a funeral director called me back asking me to pull out of a funeral he had just asked me to take. The motive was quite simple: given the family's political views, they did not feel comfortable having a black man taking the funeral of their loved one. Despite the funeral director's repeated apologies, the unwavering support of my incumbent and my own wish to gracefully bow out of the situation, I was left with a sense of numbness and a frustration I did not know how to vent.

Being a black minister had, until then, been an asset in my interaction with the community. The novelty my ethnicity brought opened the way to stirring conversations about my own background and, more significantly, about faith and the Church. Many of those I spoke to had lived most of their lives in the village or in similar contexts. To hear that I had lived in four different countries, spoke several languages and yet had chosen to move into their village was both amusing and puzzling to some. I recall a comment from one of the parishioners in a local watering hole suggesting that only two things could have brought me to Staplehurst: a momentary lapse of reason, or that I had something big to hide (referring to the fact that Staplehurst was one of the key locations in Britain's biggest ever cash robbery in February 2006). To which I responded that to any question, my standard answer was Jesus.

Jesus was the reason I found myself in Staplehurst. More significantly, Jesus was the reason I chose to lead the life I led. Vocation was not a quest for the familiar. Faith was not essentially about seeking and finding comfort for myself, but seeking and finding God in all aspects of life; it was about making God more real, more believable.

I later realized that most of our rhetoric on faith, vocation and mission can only be proven when tested. It was therefore essential for me to encounter this painful aspect of ministry. It brought home to me the fact that ministry is not always exercised from a place of strength and comfort. Often, ministry will expose our vulnerability and take us to places we would rather avoid.

Interestingly, my experience of woundedness allowed me to listen with a new-found intent to the stories that parishioners were willing to share. In listening to accounts of their lives, I discovered that my story was not an isolated one, but the story of God's people in its entirety. Those I was called to minister to carried a variety of crosses, some ugly and painful, and most of them the fruit of broken relationships. This, to me, meant that my calling was about entering into a relational experience that would ultimately make room for all to share their story, and in doing so to find healing.

Being an agent of reconciliation sounded like a worthwhile vocation. But that prospect presented me with a considerable challenge: how do I speak of reconciliation in an increasingly polarized world? How can I hold together the offender and the offended? More specifically, how do I minister to those who reject my ministry because of who I am? How do I learn to say with integrity, 'Though we are many, we are one body'?

The answer came when I eventually had the opportunity to meet the son of the woman whose funeral I had been denied the privilege of conducting. I had just finished saying morning prayer in church when a gentleman came to me, signalling that he wanted a word. After an initial hesitation he introduced himself to me. I was eager to listen to what he had to say and share some of my own thoughts. After listening to him, I was moved by the courage and integrity of his initiative. His openness allowed me in turn to be open and share my own brokenness with him. The minister had been ministered to.

Our disagreement may not have been fully bridged there and then, but I realize now that, in the safety of that place of worship, something much deeper than I could ever perceive had happened. As we stood there listening to each other's woundedness, we were able to recognize and value our respective humanity. From the collision of our two lives a spark was born, carrying with it the promise of healing and reconciliation. Sometimes, that promise is all that is needed.

So, how do I speak of reconciliation when I see myself as the aggrieved party? It seemed to me that part of the answer resides in the exploration and rediscovery of our shared humanity. In the context of my ministry, it also implied re-evaluating what it meant for me to be called Anglican. Coming from a Nonconformist background, the notion of a worldwide communion resonated with my own aspiration of a less segregated Christian identity. The Anglican effort to hold diverging views in creative tension offered me a sense that Christian identity and vocation are to be understood less as an institution, and more like a dynamic body where all find an opportunity to become 'neighbour' to the other. Being Anglican is all about being Christian in relation. Being an Anglican minister is being a minister committed to sustain vital relationships between individuals, especially when the odds do not justify such commitment.

The phenomenon of globalization is shaping our societies in such a way that most of our communities are being transformed from an organic self-understanding to a more mixed and fragmented one. Most of us as we minister will increasingly be confronted with greater cultural and ethnic diversity. Often this will be experienced in a personal, contentious and divisive fashion. It is therefore imperative for us to relentlessly seek practical outcomes that will allow us to offer avenues for healing and reconciliation.

Ministry in a Kentish village has shaped my sense of identity in more ways than I could express. In choosing to inhabit a space of mutuality and dialogue, I experienced an expansion of my own mental universe. In offering the ministry of reconciliation to others, I was allowed to experience reconciliation for and with myself. As I prepared to move away from this rich and fruitful curacy, I was able to say with confidence that it had not all been downhill from the initial three weeks. As a matter of fact, the landscape of ministry is a varied one. The mountain-top experiences only make sense when viewed alongside the wanderings in the valleys.

8

Bruce Goodwin

———•◦•———

Bruce is currently Senior Chaplain to the University of Gloucestershire. He came later to ordained ministry, having spent time as a secondary school English teacher in Perth, Western Australia, and doing mission work with Youth with a Mission in Hawaii, the Cook Islands and India. He taught EFL in London and Cheltenham and more recently for nine years in Muscat, Oman before returning to the UK to train at Trinity College, Bristol. Bruce served his three-year curacy in Thornbury benefice, which leans to the Anglo-Catholic tradition, but would class himself as an evangelical charismatic, influenced by Holy Trinity, Brompton and New Wine.

* * *

Tuesday morning had started like any other. I took my dog for a walk and then went to the church for morning prayer with John at half past eight. Strangely, he did not show up. This was quite unlike him, as in the seven months since he had moved to Thornbury he was very unlikely to miss morning prayer. After waiting for about ten minutes I wandered over to the vicarage and was surprised to see the curtains drawn in the hallway. But I assumed John was unwell or had overslept, having got back late from his day off, and I went back home. It was just after a quarter past ten on that morning of Valentine's Day 2012 when the call came. Our church secretary's voice was quiet as she simply said, 'Something terrible has happened. John's gone. He's dead.'

I couldn't believe what I was hearing. How was this possible? My mind whirling, I jumped in the car and raced down to the vicarage. The police were already there, along with our PCC secretary and two work-men who had found him. We stood in the driveway, bewildered, trying to take in what had happened. He had been found dead in the hallway of the vicarage. We were to find out later that he had been murdered.

I had moved to the quiet market town of Thornbury with my family after training at Trinity College, Bristol in the summer of 2009. We had been told at college that it was best to choose our curacy by the person we would be working with. In a variation of the famous phrase coined by Bill Clinton – 'It's the economy, stupid' – we were advised when it came to selecting a curacy: 'It's the *incumbent*, stupid.' This is a good rule of thumb. So I was not too uneasy. I had got on quite well with my prospective incumbent, the Revd David Primrose, whenever we had met and the 'arranged marriage' held relatively few fears. In our 15 months together this proved to be true.

David and I worked well together and he taught me everything I didn't know about the Church of England. Thornbury is a typical, traditional, mainstream benefice with an older congregation. Covering the nine-month vacancy after David left was not too arduous as the parish is well organized and the PCC and my senior churchwarden (a retired police officer) made every effort to help me run things. This was to prove invaluable in what was to follow.

The Revd John Suddards (previously at Witham in Essex) was appointed as David's successor and came to the parish in July 2011. John and I were very different characters and it became clear fairly early on that we were of different theological persuasions. However, I respected and appreciated John and we got on fine. He was approaching sixty, so this was probably his last parish. He had been a barrister and his sharp intellect and astute mind came to the fore as he set about his ministry. He left me free to do the things that he felt I was good at and gave me the chance to explore chaplaincy work for a month in a Bristol prison, which was enormously interesting.

As 2011 became 2012, I began to think of moving on and John was planning changes. We both wanted to see some reordering done and I was given the opportunity to start a new, informal morning service in the neighbouring village of Oldbury. The benefice was getting to know John after six months and coming to appreciate his ministry.

But what happened that cool February morning was to shape my life over the months that followed. I was on the spot and just had to deal with everything. Initially, in the hours that followed the finding of John's body, the police were in evidence. I can honestly say that they were brilliant and it is to their credit that they responded so fast. Within 24 hours they had established it was murder and within a week had caught the man. Our senior churchwarden helped considerably in how we as a church dealt with the police. I had to give a statement (which takes ages) and have fingerprints and DNA taken, as of course I had spent time in the vicarage and needed to be ruled out of their enquiries.

After the police, it was then dealing with the press, as naturally this made front-page news. This is when the diocese swung into action. The diocesan communications officer was absolutely amazing. She handled the media and took the pressure off me and the church. (My mobile phone rang constantly but I could thankfully refer the press to her every time, though I had to tell my wife and children not to answer the door or the phone for a few days.) Senior members of the diocesan staff were quickly on the scene. We went ahead with the weekly communion service the next day and the Bishop of Tewkesbury did the interviews. Interestingly, most of the press were very respectful and tried to be sensitive to our situation.

My ultimate responsibility lay with caring for, and supporting, the dozens of church members who were, like me, in shock. The questions began to surface. How can this have happened . . . ? And here? Reportedly, there hadn't been a murder in Thornbury for over 200 years. Fear and numbness were the overriding emotions and people came together whenever they could. On Friday night the Bishop of Gloucester led a memorial communion service in Thornbury Baptist Church because our own church was still a crime scene. There were over 400 people at the service and it drew the community, both Christian and wider, much closer.

For me as the curate, the event was nerve-racking. I had to do my first live television interview before the service. I stuck to the script that the communications officer and I had worked out with ITV beforehand and it seemed to go fine. As I was representing the Church generally I was acutely aware not to say anything that would be seen as stupid, controversial or unhelpful. The service passed in a blur and the bishop did a great job. We also held a vigil one week after John's death – scores of people came out for that. On Sunday morning, we allowed the press (and the police) to sit in the congregation but no cameras were allowed inside the church. I had had very little time to prepare a sermon but I really sensed God's presence as I shared my own thoughts and feelings (which many others related to) and reaffirmed our shared hope that, despite the manner of John's violent death, he was now safe in the arms of Jesus. We then entered a time of mourning.

By Ash Wednesday, eight days on, we heard that the man had been charged with murder. I had begun to see people individually and set up a series of 'teas' at our house to talk and pray with groups of people who were feeling John's loss the most. We addressed questions like, 'Where is God in all this and how can he have allowed this to happen?' There are no easy answers, but we saw John's death very much as a sacrificial one, for it is possible to say he died 'in the line of duty', seeking to reach out to someone who needed God's love.

I also went into the local Church of England school. Thankfully it had been half-term, but the school is very close to the vicarage and some were still feeling afraid. We did a combined assembly with parents and children, which was important, and I stayed and talked at length to a number of the parents over coffee. There were more press interviews to do and the Easter programme to organize, so I found myself thrust back into 'vacancy mode' once again.

Finally, after almost seven weeks, we were able to have John's funeral, on the Saturday just before Palm Sunday. I had spoken to John's sister (John was single) on the phone and amazingly he had left instructions for his funeral. Again, the diocese organized the service, which was very powerful and offered a degree of closure for us as a whole parish. I remember feeling a deep sense of relief as the hearse drew away from the parish church and we were able to say goodbye to John and begin to move on.

My curacy has become largely defined by the 'Thornbury Vicarage Murder'. Other things that happened during the curacy have receded into the background. Obviously, I never expected anything like this to happen during my time as a curate but, regardless, you have to play the hand you are dealt and get on with it as best you can. Learning to deal with the police and the press were invaluable lessons, and receiving the support of the diocese and seeing them step up to the plate so effectively was gratifying. Not all dioceses are the same, but the responsibility in these very unusual circumstances should not fall on the shoulders of the curate. Similarly, the churchwardens have a vital part to play and in my case I can say I was very ably supported throughout. I felt spiritually buoyed up by people's prayers, and received many supportive text messages.

However, I found the entire episode emotionally gruelling and felt the need for some time off after it. (Again the diocese was very generous in seeing that I had the finance for a decent break.) To be quite honest, I think it has helped the growth of my ministry. Why do I say that? Well, basically, if you can deal with something like this, you can probably deal with anything. In addition, it possibly helped me in the process of applying for my current position.

Almost two years on from the murder, two things stand out for me as I look back on it. First is the issue of how we as the clergy deal with suffering. This continues to be a hot topic. I have wrestled with the question a lot and candidly I think *every* curate must do this. Second, the world really wants to see how the Church reacts in times of great suffering. I recall a deep conversation I had with a regional reporter at the time. Essentially, this was the question he was asking: 'How do we as the Church react to tragedy – especially when it is so personal?' If we can go some way to addressing this question honestly then our credibility may increase. Lastly it should be said that leadership is the key in a situation like this, and to my mind this should be part of any curacy, especially towards the end. When a vacancy occurs during curacy, this needs to be seen as an opportunity, and, when unexpected things happen, God's grace can be sufficient. Ultimately I believe Romans 8.28, that 'in *all* things God works for the good of those who love him', and that he uses all the things that happen to us, especially in our curacies, to train and shape us – even the worst of things.

9

Ruth Fitter

Ruth is a full-time stipendiary curate. Prior to ordination, she worked as a primary school teacher, and as a family support worker for the Child and Family Court Advisory Support Service in Gloucestershire. She trained for ordination on the West of England Ministerial Training Course in Cheltenham and was ordained in Gloucester Cathedral in 2011. Her church experience ranges from the Baptist tradition to the Anglo-Catholic and she is currently serving her title within a team of churches on the edge of Cheltenham. Ruth is a member of Women and the Church and has recently taken up the role of Young Vocations Champion for the diocese. She is also the Diocesan Chaplain for the Mothers' Union.

* * *

It was about five o'clock in the evening when I finished my appointment at work and checked my phone. There I saw that I had four missed calls from my prospective training incumbent and I immediately found myself wondering what was wrong. This was in December, prior to being made deacon the following July, and to all intents and purposes the curacy was signed, sealed, announced, and – as long as I could finish the essays on time and get through the bishop's interview – hopefully delivered too. However, later that evening, I found myself sitting opposite my training incumbent being told that God's call had encouraged him to apply for a position in the diocese! If, following interview the next week, he was successful my curacy would be unable to take place in that particular parish. We would be back to the drawing board. The following week the call came to say that God and the bishop thought alike – the diocesan position was now filled by my training incumbent and I therefore needed to get in touch with the DDO rather swiftly to find another curacy.

To say I was cross would be an understatement. We'd looked at the house, my husband and children were planning to work in the area we would be moving to and I had already, after several months of thought, prayer and discussion, begun to invest emotionally in the parish. Suddenly, all of what we thought would be taking place had been taken away and we needed to start again.

Suffice to say that a new parish was found (next door to the one where we originally thought we would be) due to the generous and hugely pastoral heart of my new training incumbent and also, in part, due to my ability to calm down, be gracious and keep my heart open to the will of God – just as my potential training incumbent had done when he applied for the diocesan position.

Looking back I can see that God 'nearly' got me to the right place, but that some nudging was needed to make sure I was definitely in the right place to serve him and his people. I remember feeling rather unsettled during the autumn and couldn't work out why, but if I'm honest I knew the potential curacy was not 100 per cent – or even 96 per cent – right for me, but it is very difficult to say something like this when everyone else around you thinks it's great. It was only when I went to look round the church where I am now, and I decided to stand behind the altar – ostensibly to see if anything happened – that I had my 'Holy Spirit moment'. Suddenly, this felt like it was absolutely the right place to be. In that moment, the tangible presence of God was in the stones and the air – in me. It was a deeply affirming experience and one, looking back, that I think I needed, given all that had happened.

Discerning God's will for our ministry and for where we are to serve our curacy can be hugely difficult when so many others around us, from college tutors, spouses, family, friends and work colleagues to other clergy and potential parishioners, are all adding their advice – their voice. But it is important to have the self-awareness, and the courage, to say, 'This doesn't feel right', if it doesn't. Spending time with God alone – however you might do that (I find washing up and walking are good opportunities) – is vital to this discernment so that the other voices can be silenced for a while and the still, small voice of God can be heard above the clamour of our busy lives. So much of ministry is about having the discipline to listen to God despite all the distractions that come our way.

It has particularly been in pastoral work that this sense of 'being in the right place' has been confirmed in my curacy. It has been a real privilege to be involved in the lives of people in the parish and in their own journeys with God. When I first started my curacy in the leafy suburbs of Cheltenham many people commented, 'There'll be no problems here', perpetuating the myth that if you are middle class and seem to have a decent income and the material possessions of life then all must be well emotionally, psychologically and spiritually. This is certainly not always the case – not in my experience anyway. Many of the struggles that people are enduring go unseen day by day. Into those struggles – the real-life stories of people in the parish – has come my own faith and life story which has, quite honestly, been a real surprise to those people. It has been a surprise because they have found a fallible human being beneath the dog collar, someone who left God behind for a while and went her own way, and in so doing had to return and trust God once again in the brokenness of life.

One particular woman stands out in my mind. She was not a regular churchgoer, but she liked to sit in the church from time to time. I think she enjoyed the peace and quiet. We would bump into one another as the months went by and eventually she trusted me enough to open up about herself, because during those months we just talked generally about life and how difficult it was to have a faith of any kind when life didn't seem to be going in the direction we wanted. Eventually she contacted me to ask if we could talk in more depth, and so we did. As I listened to her, I found myself in a sense listening to my own story. There was a real connection between us. Here was a woman with whom I shared some 'life themes' – hurt and loss, a need to be loved, a constant searching for 'happiness' in ways that were not healthy for me until I realized that it was my relationship with God that would ultimately give me the happiness I craved.

That our stories were similar was a huge surprise to the woman who sat opposite me, but – vitally and wonderfully – *in my own story she could see that God was in her story*. It was quite a revelation for her, and I found it very moving to be used by God in this way. She hadn't expected to find someone who understood, especially in the Church, and that has been my experience with many other people I have spent time with. My reflection is that I have been in the right place for my curacy simply because I have been able to share my particular story with people and in the process hold out to them hope in a God who comes to sit with us in our brokenness. If we are able to offer something of our own stories to others – without burdening them – then this can establish a relationship of trust in which possibilities about faith and hope can be explored. There is something very powerful about sharing stories. It helps us to connect with others at a deep level and to discern God's presence and work in their – and our – lives. Ultimately, I think we need to be real with people and not pretend that life is a breeze, or that we are somehow perfect and holy just because we are wearing the dog collar.

I have learnt a great deal during my curacy and I have to say that this is due in large measure to the very wise training incumbent with whom I have had the privilege to work. It goes without saying that this is a key relationship, one well worth nurturing. In particular, I have come to appreciate that being a curate allows you to say and do things (and make mistakes!) that incumbents probably cannot. As a curate, I have space and time to come up with ideas and put them into action. These include the Community Advent Calendar – which is, very simply, a board outside the church with a different picture and simple text for each day of Advent, retelling the story of the first Christmas. We used it so that passers-by would maybe think twice about the real meaning of Christmas. I also get to do the more rewarding parts of the job, such as going to local schools more often, leading events such as 'Experience Easter', spending more time visiting or in the nursing home. And I'm generally able to do all of this without needing to explain why it is happening, as my training incumbent will have given me the nod of approval to go ahead. A good curacy should give us sufficient freedom to explore our gifts and calling. For an incumbent the responsibility for the overall running of the church is far greater, and there can be more emphasis on process, meetings and finance, and perhaps less chance to try new things out. After all, if the curate tries something and it doesn't work then it can always be put down to a 'training and learning experience'. I think there is, happily, more scope to 'have a go at things' as a curate. My advice is to seize the opportunity and go for it. You may just discover something more about who God is calling you to be, and come across a new area of gifting that may not have occurred to you. Being a curate can be quite an adventure!

I have also found that, because ultimately I am not in charge of the church and therefore, by implication, its spiritual trajectory, people are more accepting of me challenging them in preaching. I have felt a real freedom to express and develop some of my passions in this area. One of these is the subject of equality, which I believe underpins justice. I have been able to speak about the episcopacy of women, and about the place of women in other cultures, in the context of sermons, presentations and general conversations with a freedom that may not – I sense – always be available to incumbents.

Sometimes, however, curacy can also mean we get a glimpse of what it is like to have responsibility without authority. One month after my ordination to the priesthood, and a year into my curacy, my training incumbent was suddenly taken ill. He underwent emergency surgery and was off work for the best part of five months. Suddenly, I was presiding and preaching at every service, taking weddings and funerals, baptizing children and essentially making day-to-day decisions about the running of the parish. A bit of a steep learning curve, to say the least! I lost count of the number of people who told me that now they understood why God had placed me here, because I was in place as a priest and that enabled the church community to continue in its worship and witness. People were very kind and commented on how well I was coping with everything, although I had wonderful support from the churchwardens and others. God, however, had a huge lesson for me to learn, and that was to do with humility.

I had to learn that I could not carry out ministry solely in my own strength but only with the grace and power of God. Initially, following my incumbent's sudden illness, I ran on adrenaline. I would be in the parish office at 6.30 a.m. and go through until 10 p.m. trying to do the job of two people. I was still trying to be 'the curate' who got involved in aspects of ministry that the incumbent was unable to take on, but at the same time I was trying to hold the place and the people together in an aura of calm that enabled them to come to terms with their shock at the incumbent's illness and their own loss.

This, of course, could not continue indefinitely, and nor was it a good model of incarnational ministry, either for the parishioners or for my family. At its heart incarnational ministry is about being rather than doing. By running around like a headless chicken I could not 'be' with people enough to hear what they really wanted to say to me. And I was going to burn myself out if I carried on in this way. I was trying to make day-to-day decisions about the running of the church, matters such as the regular services, the occasional offices and the graveyard enquiries, but really had no authority to make decisions. I was not the incumbent and neither was I curate-in-charge. Eventually I realized, after one too many sleepless nights and finding I wasn't thinking clearly about how to respond to pastoral situations, that my real job was to maintain the church's equilibrium and carry through the projects that were already planned – and that for this to happen I had to lose my sense of 'importance'. I had to gain some humility instead.

What I also had to learn was that God is in charge and not me! I came to realize that in my calling I have been invited to be a co-creator of the new creation with God. This means that I am not the creator – that the coming of God's kingdom does not solely depend upon me, but upon *me and God*. Of course, I knew all of this logically, but sometimes God shows us afresh, quite vividly, what we thought we knew so well. I hope that this message of humility will stay with me and run through my ministry in the years to come, for I feel it is the only way to minister without becoming stressed or burning out (there are plenty of clergy to which that happens). But it can be a constant struggle to remember.

Curacy also involves taking on a new role and identity, even if it doesn't mean taking on a new place. Wherever and however our ministry as a curate is shaped, there is an 'ontological shift' that occurs at ordination. This means that there is a real sense that *who I am* has changed. After ordination, we can never go back to being the people we were, but instead we become 'set apart' for God. I think the 'ontological shift' is the moment when you realize that you are *in* the world but you are called to be no longer wholly *of* the world. It is the moment when something almost indescribable in the very core of your being changes. It is the moment when you fully realize that when people look at you they will see 'the Church'. It is the moment when you realize that, however supportive others have been with you on the journey so far, they cannot accompany you on this part. It is the moment when you realize that, however much you are loved by someone else, however much you love that person in return, he or she will never fully understand what it means to be ordained and ultimately 'different'. My advice is to really think this through – perhaps with others – because to be ordained is to somehow change *who you are* – and that happens in public, in full view of family, friends and parishioners. It's quite an undertaking, though it's also an incredibly exciting privilege.

People who know me well have commented that since ordination I am much calmer, more centred and seemingly more at peace with myself than I used to be. I think that is to do with a constant sense of God's presence in my core being and in all that I do which was simply not there before. My prayer is that I may take this peace and sense of God's presence into my ministry so that God's love and peace can be shared with others. Being ordained priest has brought with it a sense of completion in *who I am*. There is a real sense of coming home, but not to rest. The journey is not yet complete (in fact it seems to have just started!) and there is lots of work to do. I feel that to be ordained is to carry the privilege and responsibility of being a bearer of hope, love and light to a world in darkness. It's quite a charge, but I honestly can't think of anything else I would rather do.

Now I'm about to enter my third year of curacy, and with an unexpected house move looming, I have come to understand that ministry is never exactly what we expect it to be. There are many surprises along the way, some wonderful and some challenging: from walking into the local hospice expecting to minister to a dying patient only to find you leave a different person because they have ministered to you, to the fact that your role or home has changed suddenly. It is all part of the intricate tapestry that God is weaving. God is indeed the God of Surprises; the God who calls us to leave what we know, to leave the familiar behind and to take a risk. My final piece of advice? Listen to God's call and go for it!

10

Rob Kean

———◦◦◦———

Rob is a full-time stipendiary curate. Prior to ordination, he worked in IT for ten years, latterly as technical IT operations manager for a teaching union, but has also worked as a London cab driver. He trained for ordination at St Mellitus College in London and was ordained in Chelmsford Cathedral in 2011. He is currently serving his curacy in two churches, one in the Anglo-Catholic tradition and the other a Local Ecumenical Partnership of the Church of England, Methodist, Baptist and United Reformed Church in a central worship tradition.

* * *

'*Vicar in the house!*' – that's the warning cry of the landlord of my local pub when I pop in, normally every Thursday (with Friday being my day off, it's a nice way to 'end' the week). I think the 'warning' was started by the landlord as a light-hearted way to get people to tone down their language. Not that they do – or rather, if what I am hearing *is* the toned-down version, I would hate to hear the untoned-down. In any event, there is no chance of being anonymous in the local pub or enjoying a quiet pint, not with an entrance like that!

I can't remember making a conscious effort to get involved with the 'unchurched' of the parish. I just decided when we moved here that I would do the things that I enjoy, and be myself with the people I met. So I also joined the local short mat bowls club, which was a new activity for me but something I wanted to try. I thought it might be fun and a good way to meet a new community of people, although a few of the regulars at the pub have questioned my motives for taking up bowls. They suggest it's a way of 'getting customers' for funerals – the bowls club having a slightly older age profile than the parish as a whole!

I have found that getting to know people who don't come to church has been one of the most rewarding aspects of my curacy so far. The Church of England gives its ordained ministers a wonderful remit, that they should share in the 'cure of souls' for the whole parish, not just the people that walk through the doors on a Sunday. I find this rewarding because it gives me the opportunity to engage with and be available for people in the parish who otherwise wouldn't have much connection with the church. It's about me going to them and meeting them where they are. I see mission and evangelism as more of a long-term prospect. Our diocese is currently having a mission drive for its centenary focus, and one of the statistics that has had an impression on me is that for about 75–80 per cent of people, their faith journey takes an average of five years, as opposed to a sudden conversion. That being the case, I think it is important to be alongside people who don't attend church as opposed to preaching only to the converted.

Going into any new place for the very first time is always a little daunting, I find, and going into a village pub is possibly not the most inviting of prospects. I deliberately didn't wear my dog collar for my first visit to the pub because it was (and still is) primarily a social visit, but this being a small village I had a fair idea that at least a few people would know who the newcomer was. Word soon gets round about the identity of the new vicar (and probably what he or she is like!).

There can be a tension of sorts when you are a recognizable person belonging to any institution in a public place, whether a police officer or a vicar. I guess that's why both of those roles are a 'calling' rather than just a job. For example, if you are a policeman it wouldn't be right for you to neglect something occurring in a pub environment that was illegal. It's similar in my experience as a clergyman. There have been times when I have heard racist or sexist comments, or seen plain bully-ing in one form or another, and the trick I think is not *what* to say in these situations, but often *how* to say it and possibly *when*.

On one of those occasions when the landlord decided to announce my presence – 'Steady, we have a vicar in the building' – in order to curb the regulars' language, the reply that came back from one of the punters was, 'At least I am not a paedophile!' It was quite a shocking thing to be said in a public place, and it happened early on in my curacy, when I had only been in the pub a couple of times. Charming, I thought! Now, I do have quite a bit of life experience but – if I am honest – it knocked my confidence a little. I did not know the person concerned, and it made me wonder whether or not my visits to the pub should continue. My reflection is that when we are newly ordained we can feel vulnerable from time to time because we are growing into and learning about our new public role. But continue I did, and with-in a couple of weeks I was having in-depth conversations with that very same person about all sorts of things. Perhaps the remark came about from losing face after being publicly rebuked by the landlord, or from a need to be one of the lads, or perhaps he thought 'vicars' are fair game when it comes to public ridicule . . . Whatever it was, it's often the case that I don't need to spring to my own defence – there's always someone willing to tell the offender on your behalf to pipe down.

It is true that the simple presence of someone ordained can cause all sorts of reactions. So we should not underestimate the possibility of ministry by our presence. In who we are and what we represent we may quietly challenge the people we come into contact with to ask questions, to think about some of the big questions in life, even to modify their behaviour. I remember a conversation with a pub customer one evening:

PUB CUSTOMER: I think you coming in here has been a calming influence.
ME: What makes you say that?
PUB CUSTOMER: Well, since I have known you, I haven't hit anyone.
ME: That's good then.

Not being a frequenter of pubs before starting my curacy (honest, Bishop!), I had no idea of how typical my local pub is, but it seems that everyone who is a regular there has a nickname. It might indeed be said that you can only count yourself a regular if you have attained this badge of honour. My reflection is that at a deeper level, this says something about belonging and acceptance in the pub community. There's no opportunity to choose your nickname; it is something bestowed on you by the pub landlord. After some time I plucked up the courage to ask if I had a nickname, and I learned that I am generally referred to as 'Halo Bob' (it could be worse, trust me!) – although there is one person who refers to me as Gregory Peck (as seen in the film *The Omen*). I like having a nickname because to me it says that I am accepted in the community.

Being a curate has also led to some strange (well, they were to me) requests to bless people in the pub. I remember meeting a gentleman who was getting married the next day. He and his wife were having a civil ceremony, and he asked if I could pray for him. Of course I would, I said, making a mental note to pray for him and his wife-to-be when I next prayed. But no, he meant there and then, in the middle of a crowded pub! Obviously I obliged. The other time that this happened wasn't in my local but at a baptism reception in another pub. I had my clerical shirt and collar on, and I walked up to the bar to get a drink. Before I could say anything, the barmaid asked if I would bless her, again there and then – of course, now I was a dab hand at on-the-spot blessings and prayers. There are also a couple of people in the pub who seem to think that buying me a drink is some kind of modern-day practice of indulgences, and that it will notch up a few points for them with God.

As I reflect on my ministry, what stands out for me are the many pastoral encounters. When people get to know and trust you, I have found, all they want to do is tell you something of their life story, and to be accepted for who they are as opposed to the person they think they need to be. And when I show them unconditional acceptance, I sense that they feel that the Church and ultimately God accepts them too – and this is very important for them to know. My wife Angela and I recently went to a New Year's Eve party at the house of some friends from the pub, and the host said a couple of times that evening, 'You see, we are good people really.' Accepting an invitation into someone's home is showing them that you accept them into your heart – it's somehow akin to saying that they are worthy. My advice is, the next time you or I refuse an invitation, we might pause for a moment to think about the upset it could be causing.

It's difficult for me to speak of the precise nature of some pastoral conversations for fear of breaking confidentiality, but they can include marriage problems, the guilt of unfinished business when a loved one dies, depression, worries about their children . . . all the things that you would hear about in the church. Life is pretty much the same outside it as well.

Spending time in public, social situations such as the pub can help us to understand the community in which we are called to serve. Part of this is to do with discerning how people are connected. I have found that the connections when you live in a village can be quite staggering. The house I live in was once owned by 'Twice a day Dave's' son ('twice a day every day' is his nickname because that's how often he is in the pub!). The current owner of the house (it is rented by the diocese) is the cousin of the person who asked me to pray for his marriage, and his best friend was the person who put all the windows and doors in the house. At the first wedding I officiated at, the bride was the cousin of one of the bar staff, and I recently found out that someone who I have been friends with at the pub for some time is the husband of a fellow school governor (having known them both in those separate capacities for a while). All of this helps us to discern 'micro-communities' and understand how different groupings of people are formed and relate to the wider community. My advice is that if you really want to understand the community in which you live or work, then you must 'get out there' in order to meet people and start to listen to their stories. We will never get to know and be fully accepted by our community if we hide within the church walls.

It really is an honour and privilege to know the people in the parish, to be part of their lives and ultimately to serve them in any way that I can – whether they ever set foot in the church or not. I do not believe there is such a thing as the 'unchurched' – let's agree to call them the 'not churched yet'. During ordination training, one of the texts we read was Avery Dulles's *Models of the Church*. I am sure we curates all have our own take on the different models included in the book, but I would like to think that one of the models I take to heart is referred to as 'the Church as Servant'. This 'asserts that the Church should consider itself as part of the total human family, sharing the same concerns as the rest of men', and that 'Just as Christ came into the world not to be served but to serve, so the Church, carrying on the mission of Christ, seeks to serve the world' (p. 91). It may seem a strange way of serving, but being with the people where they are and how they are, and in particular hearing their stories, is for me the best starting point.

Getting involved with the community in which you are placed should also never be a forced or unnatural thing. If you are not comfortable with a pub environment, or if bowls is not your thing, then I am not suggesting that you 'take up your cross for the sake of the gospel' and force yourself to go. That wouldn't be good news. You will have things that you enjoy doing and people that you will naturally spend time with through various activities. If you have children at school, for example, much of what you do socially will be based around them. Do what feels right and just be yourself. I have found that people have responded to *me being genuinely me*. There is little point in trying to be anyone else – people will see through you quite quickly!

I don't go in for selling the gospel as such. What I mean by that is, I have no intention whatsoever when I go into the pub of telling people about Christ. For me, if I have to sell something, to push it on people, then it is not worth having in the first place. The gospel message is something worth having, of course it is, but I have found that it doesn't need the hard sell, because given the opportunity people will talk to you about it and ask questions. Being ordained (whether we wear the dog collar or not) means that we are available for conversations about God and faith and the Church. It comes with the job and sometimes it's unavoidable. In fact I often hope for a proper break from 'work' when I walk into the pub, but with the landlord shouting 'Vicar in the house' it seldom happens.

In a review of the book *How to Be a Bad Christian and a Better Human Being* by Dave Tomlinson I came across a line that I love: 'A vicar in the pub is worth two in a pulpit.' It demonstrates a key point for me about incarnational ministry, which is at the heart of my vocation to ordained ministry. It's all about meeting people where they are and how they are – just as Jesus did. Ministry is not just about what we do in church (as important as that is), it's about how we are good news in the whole of our community. How do we – as ordained ministers – proclaim the gospel in a relevant and accessible way? What questions and feelings do we stir up by our presence? Where are the places in our communities that are as yet untouched by the gospel? These are questions that I am continuing to grapple with. And in the meantime I shall continue to visit the pub on a Thursday and we shall see what further surprises God has in store. Which reminds me, I am still trying to get my bar tab accepted as a legitimate ministerial expense by my PCC, but no luck so far. We do, however, live in hope!

11

Jacqueline Stober

Jacqueline is a full-time stipendiary curate. Prior to ordination, she taught special-needs children, juniors and secondary science. She trained for ordination on the Northern Ordination Course and was ordained in 2007. Jacqueline came to faith as a child in an evangelical church, but feels most at home in the liberal Anglo-Catholic tradition. For many years she lived in the USA and Canada, where her own children were born. She served two suburban curacies and was a General Synod representative. She is now vicar of Denton, Newcastle.

* * *

I was sick in bed with flu when the archdeacon rang to say my training incumbent had died suddenly that morning.

Thinking back to that day it seems as though the whole of my ministry focuses on that moment; everything either leading up to it, or leading away from it. You know how a fridge works? Air is forced from a small space into a larger one through a tiny hole, and the rapid expansion of gas causes a drop in temperature. From being unfocused and idealistic in the cosiness of theological study, suddenly I found myself alone, thrust into a rather harsh world, very different from where I'd expected to be, learning lessons about myself I'd rather not.

It was a large and busy parish. I'd chosen the post deliberately because of the heavy workload. I didn't feel as though I'd had enough experience during training and I wanted to be well prepared to lead my own parish. I'd picked a placement that seemed to offer as rich a range of training opportunities as possible. The previous curate warned me that if I took up the post I'd hit the ground running; how true that turned out to be.

I moved into the curate's house on a high. I couldn't believe it; they put me in a clerical collar and paid me to study the Bible, pray and share the gospel. Initially a bit hesitant about my being a woman and black, people mostly got over it. The parish had everything: weddings, baptisms, funerals, uniformed organizations, Sunday school, Mothers' Union, schools work, nursing homes, Bible studies. I liked the rapport between the reader and the vicar, and looked forward to being a part of their team; daily morning and evening prayer together meant a time for reflection and fellowship at the beginning and end of every day, just about everything a curate could wish for.

My training incumbent was amazing: a larger than life character, he could speak at length about virtually any subject you could name, and because both he and the reader were so experienced, it was daunting preaching alongside them. I was having problems finding my own voice in the pulpit: I didn't speak with authority, and whereas for some people matters of faith were clearly black and white, my own experience was that lived-out Christianity was often more situational.

The vicar had a reputation for being an extremely hard worker. Physically fit, he would cycle 20 miles in the morning then do a full day in the parish, often ending at half past ten when he helped clean up the hall after a social evening. In addition, he was area dean as well as chaplain to the mayor. As he was good at driving change forward, we were also the pilot for most new diocesan initiatives. I soon realized that if I was going to be a vicar one day, I would have to develop my own leadership style. Not that I was averse to hard work or risk-taking, but as the single parent of two teenagers, that breathtaking work rate for me would need to be tempered with reflection and family time.

A year after my priesting things began to change. My vicar began teaching me how to handle an interregnum. I gathered that he was applying for other posts and he was eventually successful, but before it was announced, suddenly he was gone; a heart attack on the way to the gym.

It was devastating. The whole diocese was in shock, but for his family, senior clergy and the parish the anguish was intense.

Putting my own feelings aside I set about getting on with the running of the parish. The vicar had said the reader and I should not do all the preaching but bring others in to share the load. Now, though, to keep costs down, the wardens asked us to do everything between us. I refused: I knew what the vicar had wanted. Unfortunately, what may have been intended as a kindly meant concession to my developing confidence in the pulpit was misinterpreted by the distraught wardens. My determination to stick to his original plan for the preaching rota was thought to be an attempt to direct the interregnum, be in charge and maybe even be their new vicar. Who did I think I was? His memory began to take on the aura of a saint, and as the only priest available I was no comparison. Our relationship became strained and I became the focus for their grief.

I had been in this situation before. My husband had been an ordinand but sadly, due to treatment-resistant depression, he dropped out of training. After a decade of struggling he eventually went to counselling, but his mental state became even worse. A searchlight panning the country-side, he looked for an explanation – someone or something to blame. I watched as responsibility passed from his parents, to the Church, to God, to settle on me and the children, and that's where it remained. Our marriage ended badly, but that's another story.

I adopted the previous vicar's style and focused too much on tasks. My workload rose to a 60-hour week: visiting, schools work, almost 200 funerals, dozens of baptisms and several weddings. But it wasn't enough to win their approval. Parishioners understood that we were all struggling to do our best and, while they were sympathetic, most of them moved on with their lives. I have to say that I wouldn't have survived there at all without the loyal support of some members of the church, but my relationships with the leaders stayed challenging. I know they projected their grief on to me – anger is an easier emotion than sadness – but I wasn't equipped for bereavement counselling. Roles became blurred: while I was on holiday the reader was asked to preside over a Eucharist. Although she'd not been trained, she was asked to take a large funeral for a popular university professor, rather than bring in a retired priest. In fairness to her, she was probably just anxious to help out, but I felt undervalued and undermined.

Isolated, I began to be excluded from social events, meetings and even things that as a former teacher I was gifted at, like children's work. Things went from bad to worse. Although I attended several workshops on conflict resolution and the management of change, I was powerless to improve things. From thinking of myself as being a strong, competent survivor, I was turning into a victim; it was like watching a train crash in slow motion. I needed help.

In an attempt to keep things in perspective and nurture myself I stood for election to General Synod, joined my daughter's theatre group and even learned to tap dance. A supervisor was eventually appointed but despite many coffees with friends and colleagues – yes, they listened to an awful lot of whining – 18 months later things at church still weren't much improved and I was exhausted. Finally the bishop put forward the idea of a second curacy. Generously he didn't suggest it was in any way my fault, but my formation as a priest had been interrupted. I'd be a senior curate and responsible for their Café Network. In addition I'd be in the city, where I eventually wanted to be. I was warmly welcomed by my new parish; they cared for me and encouraged me in my developing ministry and helped reassure me as to my value in the Church.

On reflection, after some initial training with a gifted incumbent, I can see how God had chosen me to be with my title parish at that difficult time specifically because of my knowledge of loss and bereave-ment. I understood the processes of mourning they were going through.

I remember a pained conversation back in the warden's vestry where it was said wistfully, almost apologetically, that the problem was that there was a leadership vacuum. Although maybe they shouldn't have hero-worshipped and become as emotionally dependent on him as they did, maybe this man's particular management style made their reaction to his loss inevitable. While all I longed for was to pastor them through that terrible time, I was unable to reach them. The church needed empathy and reassurance, but what they wanted was a CEO and I simply didn't fit the bill.

By God's grace, three years later some of those relationships are beginning to heal; I am in another diocese, and was delighted that representatives from both parishes made the long journey to my induction service. I pray for my old parish with their new vicar and curate regularly, and now that those days are far enough in the past to give me some perspective I can see several threads in my story which worked together to create the perfect storm. While I wouldn't wish the experience on anyone, I am grateful for the lessons I have learnt. Through it all I have finally found my own management style and my own voice; I lead from behind, like a shepherd among her flock, or a mother hen who walks alongside her chicks.

And preaching? One of my new parishioners told me a couple of weeks ago that she loves my sermons; it's just like having a conversation. I may be no giant in the pulpit, but at least I am being my authentic self.

Hopefully your curacy will be straightforward and affirming. Public ministry does not always take place inside a fridge, but in the warmth of God's loving care and the fellowship and approval of his people. But if you do sense the temperature beginning to fall, you really only need three things to help you through difficult times: some very good friends who will love you and affirm your gifts; a foundation of robust spiritual practices such as prayer, meditation, reflection; plus a little faith that the God who called you will sustain you no matter what life may bring.

12

David Smith

---•◆•---

David is the vicar of St George's Church, Tuffley and St Margaret's Church, Whaddon in the Diocese of Gloucester. He is also area dean for the Gloucester City Deanery. He was ordained in 2005 and served his curacy in the neighbouring parish of Matson, an urban priority area (UPA). Prior to ordination, he served for 33 years in the RAF as an engineer. He is married to Angela, who is also ordained, and they have four children.

* * *

It was a dark and stormy night – well, perhaps not stormy, but it was dark and very cold, and noisy, because it was 5 November. Angela and I were driving home mid-evening from an event in a neighbouring parish and had noticed a group of youths and children gathering by one of the bus stops, not one of their normal 'hanging out' places. A few minutes later, just before we arrived home, the local radio carried a news bulletin including an item about a road accident in the parish in which a local lad, a 15-year-old boy, had been taken away in an ambulance. At first, there was some uncertainty about his condition. However, it was soon confirmed that he had in fact died as a result of the accident.

With all of four months' experience as a deacon, still finding my way around this local UPA community, and with my training incumbent on holiday, I wasn't sure whether anything much could or should be done. Still in our normal working dress for the parish (in other words, black shirt and clerical collar) I went back to the bus stop, to find around 15 youngsters there. They were mainly teenagers, but the youngest was only about eight, even though by this time it was nearly 9 p.m. on a cold autumn night. I knew none of them by sight, but they were all looking decidedly cold and aimless, and they seemed neither interested nor bothered by my arrival. Though perhaps a little unsure as to how to start the conversation, I need not have worried – it only took a casual enquiry on my part to start almost a torrent of story-telling as to what had happened. Simple care and concern were all that was needed to gain acceptance into that temporary gathering.

63

It seemed that Bonfire Night for at least some of them had started with 'Frosty Jack' (white cider!), of which Lennie (as I'll call him for the purposes of this chapter) had had sufficient to make him stagger around, though not quite enough to render him unconscious. Put simply, two cars had been approaching from opposite directions. Lennie had tripped on the kerb and fallen into the path of the first car, which had then knocked him into the path of the other car. Though most of his injuries were survivable, the second impact had caused a skull fracture from which he never regained consciousness. All this was told several times over, in different ways by different voices, but at this stage all with the sense of unbelief that such a thing could happen to their friend.

Then the questions began. What is heaven like? Has Lennie got wings now? What happens at a funeral? What is God going to say to him when he gets there? Interestingly, in all the story-telling, Lennie's friends had made no secret of the fact that he had had a few brushes with the law – said almost with a sense of pride in his various exploits! – and yet in all the questions there was not a shadow of doubt about the existence of God or heaven, or that Lennie was already there.

Despite the alcohol, they were very quiet when we agreed that it would be good to pray for Lennie in that place – which we duly did. After about an hour with them, it felt right to return home, though many of the youngsters were reluctant to leave, despite the cold. Even if they were later gathered up by parents, they seemed determined to return the following night, to revisit the accident scene. Rather tentatively, I said I would be happy to open the church if they wanted somewhere slightly warmer to gather on the following evening. To start with they asked questions such as 'Are we allowed in?' and 'What will we have to do?', but after reassuring them that they could just come in and 'be', they were soon asking – slightly to my surprise – 'Can our friends come?' To which, of course, I said they could.

Before leaving, and with no promises on either side, I simply agreed that I would be in the church, with the heating on, at 7 p.m. the following evening, if they wanted to come and remember Lennie, and perhaps tell me some more about him. I returned home content that I had tried to reach out to them and seemed to have made some degree of connection, and that there were at least a couple, from what they had said, who were likely to come to the church.

The following day, parish life continued with morning prayer, some paperwork and a short home visit. By mid-morning, however, I was getting phone calls asking when Lennie's 'memorial service' was taking place, and it quickly became clear that the word was being spread that a special service was going to be held in the church that night. It also emerged that Lennie's family had been told, and were keen to come and be part of whatever was happening. I felt I had no option but to visit Lennie's family – albeit unannounced and uninvited – to explain the simple suggestion I had made and to make sure they were content with what now appeared to be developing.

Again, I need not have worried. They were very welcoming, despite their numbness and grief. We agreed there would be no formal service as such – just an opportunity for Lennie's friends to come to the church to remember him, perhaps to light a candle in his memory, and say some short prayers. One of his older sisters wanted to compile a CD of some of his favourite tracks which could be played – just another simple way of remembering.

As the day went on, it seemed likely that the 15 youngsters who had gathered the previous evening were planning on bringing friends and that we might end up with 30 or 40 people in church, as well as some of Lennie's family. The churchwardens were slightly apprehensive when I explained what I had offered and that we might have a number of youngsters in the church that evening, including most probably some of the known local tearaways, but they agreed to be there to help.

Apart from having tealights available, we also took some pads of Post-Its and plenty of pens, and laid some sheets of plain ceiling paper across the altar, but that was about the limit of the practical preparation at such short notice. Having suggested we would open the church at 7 p.m., I went to get things ready at about 6.15 p.m., to find 20 or so young people already gathered at the church, despite its being even colder than the previous evening! By 7 p.m., 20 had become 50, and an hour later there were over 100 in church, with everyone except me, the churchwardens and Lennie's parents being under 18.

The CD tracks weren't exactly typical church music, but then neither is much of the music at many funerals. They were, however, meaningful to these young people and evoked memories of Lennie for them. When they were being played, there was almost complete silence, except for one or two quietly sobbing; a couple towards the back of the church started talking and were very quickly told by those around them to be quiet and 'show some respect'. One or two who arrived either smoking or with a can of lager in hand (or both) were also 'dealt with' by Lennie's friends and told firmly what they could and could not do in 'their' church. In the end, the churchwardens sat at the back and – to their surprise – marvelled at over 100 young people very effectively 'policing' their own.

We invited them all to light a candle in Lennie's memory and, if they liked, to write a message or thought on one of the Post-Its. There was a great sense of reverence and order as candles were then placed on the votive stand – which was quickly filled – and the notes were stuck to the sheets of paper across the altar, together with more candles. Within a few minutes, the sanctuary was filled with candlelight, and Lennie's friends had effectively created a whole new multi-coloured altar frontal from their handwritten notes. We had also been joined by two of the staff from the local ecumenical youth project, and the whole atmosphere seemed to promote conversations on issues of life and faith which simply didn't surface in the normal day-to-day lives of these youngsters. In the end, the CD was played several times over, with some prayers said in the quiet spaces. It was nearly 10 p.m. when the last of our visitors finally felt able to leave, many having stayed for over three hours, and not just because it was cold outside.

Reading this, you may be tempted to start applying excessively long theological adjectives to some of the events, or analysing them in terms of the traditional models of grief and grieving. Instead, I offer only some short, simple reflections.

- In this parish, at 8 p.m. on a cold wintry night, the only 'professionals' left serving the area are the clergy. Teachers, doctors, shopkeepers, social workers, etc., are all long gone to their homes – probably well outside the area! The emergency services, when needed, are prompt and welcome – but they too are still incomers to an event and to the community, to get the job done and go away again. As clergy, we should never underestimate the value of simply living in the community we serve.

- What about the 'service' in the church? To paraphrase a *Star Trek* quote: 'It's worship, Jim, but not as we know it!' And it was significantly removed from the Sunday morning, modern Anglo-Catholic Eucharist which was our tradition. But worship it most certainly was. With just a few simple provisions, the church was able to 'be there' for these young people, who then found themselves able to explore and express their feelings about Lennie's death, and to honour him before God in a safe and creative way.

- What about being a deacon and very junior curate? Such terms meant nothing to these young people. For them, 'dog collar' equals 'vicar', and my experience on that cold dark night was that it simply identified me as representing a church presence, even though they didn't know me personally. There was an almost immediate acceptance that it was appropriate for a vicar to arrive at that place of tragedy, and with it an expectation of helping them make sense of such a senseless event. Though apprehensive at first about what – if anything – to do, I think I learned that people are quick to discern motivation. If we approach such ministry with simple human care, reflecting God's love to those we meet, this will often be of more value than anything else.

All this reminded me then, and has done ever since, that from the day we are ordained and assume the dog collar, we gain both the privilege and responsibility of representing Christ and his Church to people we have never met before and may never see again. Sometimes, we may get just a brief window of opportunity into someone else's life to make the gospel relevant. And often it will be enough to be there, keep it simple, and let God do the rest.

13

John Paul Hoskins

———————

John Paul was formerly a full-time stipendiary curate. He was ordained in 2007 and served his curacy in a beautiful rural benefice in the heart of the Peak District. The benefice includes the small market town of Bakewell as well as four other villages. John Paul trained for ordination at Ripon College Cuddesdon and before that combined postgraduate study in theology with a career as a cathedral musician. Since 2011 he has been chaplain to the Bishop of Gloucester, is an honorary minor canon of Gloucester Cathedral and also serves the national church as a bishops' selection adviser.

* * *

Rural churches are particularly closely connected with the wider life of the small communities in which they are found. Although often tight-knit, beneath the surface rural communities are diverse in character and manifest tensions that are not always immediately obvious to the outsider. Ministry in such a setting requires considerable patience and the ability to draw alongside people, but also the energy to keep lots of different plates spinning at once.

> For the beauty of the earth,
> for the beauty of the skies,
> for the love which from our birth
> over and around us lies:
> > *Lord of all, to thee we raise*
> > *this our sacrifice of praise.*

Pierpoint's well-known hymn juxtaposes thanksgiving for the beauty of creation with thanksgiving for the gift to us of God's Church. The interplay between these themes describes well my experience of rural ministry.

I didn't expect to become the curate of Bakewell, having no prior connections with Derbyshire. But when my wife got a job in Chesterfield halfway through my time at Cuddesdon, fortunately the Bishop of Derby decided to take me on. I don't think I had ever been to the Peak District before.

The key thing I was looking for in a curacy was a training incumbent I would get on with. I had seen far too many curacies that had broken down or where vicar and curate were barely on speaking terms after three years. It was very clear that Tony and I would get on well, were on the same wavelength and would be able to have fun together. This was much more important than other, more tangible factors such as church tradition or socio-economic context. It also helped that we would both be new in post. When Tony asked me to be his curate, he knew that he was going to Bakewell, but he had not yet moved. So I was able to attend his licensing, and in due course we were able to begin to figure out the parishes together. We both knew that there was some difficult recent history in Bakewell itself which would need careful disentangling, and in fact this ministry of reconciliation was very attractive as an added challenge.

But there were other specific reasons why this rural benefice felt like the right place to serve my title. Most obviously, it was an utterly lovely part of the countryside. But Bakewell was also quite similar to the small town where I grew up, so I thought that I would arrive with some prior sense of how the community might work.

Tony's long-serving predecessor had been vicar of Bakewell and Over Haddon, but pastoral reorganization meant that Tony would also be taking on the three additional villages of Ashford, Sheldon and Rowsley. There was some uncertainty about my role in all this. In any case, the diocese was moving towards encouraging larger clusters of parishes to work together in Mission and Ministry Areas (MMAs). There was some suggestion that I should have a wider brief working across all 18 parishes of the MMA. I resisted this, because I suspected that it could lead to a rather shallow curacy experience with little opportunity for real engagement anywhere.

One advantage of moving to a rural curacy was that we were to live in a spare vicarage in yet another nearby village. This was a wonderful house, and there would be little danger of being disturbed on my day off; but it did set up the expectation that I might have some involvement with the parish in which we were living. The archdeacon actually asked me, on the way into my ordination as deacon, where he should announce that I would be serving, which did not suggest that these questions had been entirely settled. It later became clear that not living in the benefice was a serious disadvantage in terms of getting to know people.

> For the beauty of each hour,
> of the day and of the night,
> hill and vale, and tree and flower,
> sun and moon and stars of light:
> > *Lord of all, to thee we raise*
> > *this our sacrifice of praise.*

The new benefice consists of five somewhat distinct communities. Bakewell is a small market town with a population of around 3,000, with one of the highest proportions of retired people anywhere in the country. It is an important service centre for the surrounding area, as well as a tourist destination in its own right. The annual agricultural show in August draws a huge number of visitors from a wide area. Bakewell includes a substantial housing estate, Moorhall, on a hill above the old town centre.

The other villages of the benefice are quite varied. Rowsley is to the south of Bakewell on the road to Matlock, and is closely associated with the estates of the Duke of Rutland: the old part of the village has a slightly feudal feel to it, but there is also an industrial estate and a small retail outlet which draws shoppers in from further afield. Ashford is a mile or two north-west of Bakewell and is one of the loveliest villages in the Peak District, with a large number of second homes and holiday lets. Over Haddon and Sheldon are small villages in the hills to the west of Bakewell, in which farming is still economically and culturally significant.

Although all of these communities are quite close-knit, particularly the smallest villages, in many cases there is something of a divide between longstanding villagers and 'outsiders'. The latter now make up the majority, with many wealthy professionals moving in and commuting to nearby towns and cities. This has driven up housing costs to the point where local people can often no longer afford to live there. Younger people are gradually having to move away, either to the more remote and less well-serviced villages, or to Chesterfield and Sheffield.

Although Bakewell is clearly the centre of gravity in the area, as the largest settlement and the place where people do their shopping, the villages define themselves to some extent as 'not Bakewell'. Thus there is a centrifugal relationship between the town and the villages. This is particularly true in connection with Ashford. In the life of the church, the situation is exacerbated by the fact that Ashford and Sheldon were previously part of a different benefice which had been split, part coming in with Bakewell and part going elsewhere, resulting in something of a sense of bereavement in those parishes. Those leading pastoral reorganization can sometimes appear on the ground like Nicolson's description of the Congress of Vienna: 'mere hucksters in the diplomatic market, bartering the happiness of millions with a scented smile'.

> For the joy of human love,
> brother, sister, parent, child,
> friends on earth and friends above,
> for all gentle thoughts and mild:
> > *Lord of all, to thee we raise*
> > *this our sacrifice of praise.*

The parish church in Bakewell inevitably dominates the life of the benefice, as the largest building in the largest community and the one with the largest congregation. The church is located on a hill, with a steep walk up from the town centre, and there was a sense when Tony and I arrived that it had become disconnected from the wider life of the town and was rather inward-looking. For a leaflet featuring a picture of the church on the hill, I suggested the deliberately tongue-in-cheek and ambiguous caption 'Bakewell church overlooks the town . . .' We wanted to make it very clear that we were open for business, and the strategy Tony and I employed was to be very visible in not taking ourselves too seriously. Much time and energy was spent on well dressings, carnival floats and in launching an annual pantomime. I have never done so much cross-dressing.

There is a strong sense of place in rural communities, which manifests itself in spirituality that is closely connected to the rhythm of the year and the immediate geography. Rural churches need to be available to all and inclusive in character. There is an equally strong expectation that the church should be there for all members of the community, whether or not people attend it regularly. The buttresses of the church, supporting it from outside, are at least as important as its pillars.

As in most other places, all five churches of this benefice have ageing congregations. Unusually, it may be that the congregations are self-sustaining to the extent that more older people keep moving to the area. Nevertheless, there is a need for collaborative, enabling leadership to release the energy of the various congregations. As more and more churches are linked together, it becomes less and less possible (even if it were ever desirable) for the clergy to do everything. But releasing energy among the laity requires a considerable input of energy in the first place from their clergy in terms of nurture and training. A few people are already doing a great number of tasks, and many of them are very involved in wider community life as well. Constantly trying to encourage the gifts of the congregation can simply become coercive when people are very busy.

An inevitable aspect of rural church life is that congregations are often very small. The two smallest churches in the benefice have regular congregations of half a dozen or fewer. This is the down side of that strong sense of rootedness in a particular place. There is considerable reluctance to travel even a mile or two to share in the wider life of the benefice. It took me a long time to realize that the corresponding advantage of small congregations is that people know each other well.

When I arrived there were far too many meetings, many of them inordinately but inevitably focused on church buildings. We experimented to create PCC sub-committees in order to free up time for more strategic thinking, but of course this meant more meetings. One solution might eventually be to move towards the creation of a single parish with a single PCC. There is currently little possibility of moving towards a 'minster' model, since there is not yet enough sense of commonality among the five churches. In the meantime, the clergy and other key individuals need to have exceptionally well-organized diaries.

In other circumstances, it might have made sense for me to have been given specific pastoral responsibility for one or two of the villages. But since Tony was also very new, it was important for him to have the opportunity to build up relationships across the benefice and to become 'the vicar' of all five communities. I had anticipated that during my deacon's year I would be able to have lots of free time to loiter with intent on the edges of the church. In practice, with complex structures and many challenges to face, I allowed myself to get sucked too quickly into the business of propping up the institution. My personal preference for being well prepared also meant that I spent too long at my desk, rather than winging it occasionally and using the space this would have freed up to get out there and be with people.

> For each perfect gift of thine,
> to our race so freely given,
> graces human and divine,
> flowers of earth and buds of heaven:
> *Lord of all, to thee we raise*
> *this our sacrifice of praise.*

Even with the declining importance of agriculture, people living in the countryside have a strong sense of the rhythm of the seasons. This means that they still come to church in large numbers at Christmas and to a lesser extent at Easter. Harvest festivals are also popular. Perhaps just as important, in terms of punctuating the turning of the year, are the annual well blessings which are an integral part of the life of many Derbyshire villages.

Week by week, the pattern of Sunday services can be a challenge. This is where the analogy of spinning plates (or of an air traffic controller landing aeroplanes) can feel most real. I believe passionately that the Church is most deeply formed by the Eucharist, but there is no doubt that in large benefices the move away from non-eucharistic worship in the last two generations has created something of a problem. I often felt like a 'mass priest', dashing from one church to the next: the pattern for the third Sunday of the month required one of us to celebrate at 9 a.m., 9.45 a.m. and 11 a.m. in three different places. It is very difficult to get to know people when on Sunday morning you are rushing in and rushing out again. The situation is compounded when the priest might only be in one of the villages on a Sunday every other month. The help of retired clergy is essential, but the people do rightly expect to see 'their' vicar (and to a lesser extent the curate).

Small congregations do not necessarily mean that all of those attending a particular church are from that village. A few people do regularly attend worship in a church other than their own. This may be for family reasons, or because they have fallen out with someone in the past, or simply because they prefer the traditional language of the 8 a.m. service. One of the smaller congregations in the benefice was almost entirely populated by exiles from elsewhere, leading to very serious doubts about the realistic possibility of any meaningful engagement with the village and the viability of the congregation. But it took me a while to realize that four people attending worship from a village of just 80 is 5 per cent of the population, which is actually not bad.

Preaching at worship was an interesting challenge. It needed to connect not only with the congregation's sense of rootedness to place, but also with the concerns of often highly educated and independently minded professionals. Rural ministry is strongly incarnational in character, needing to engage with local culture in order sometimes to challenge it.

I realized very quickly the importance of the occasional offices. Baptisms, weddings and funerals are significant moments in the life of tight-knit communities, especially when those communities are experiencing the kind of centrifugal pressures discussed above. It was vital to make the most of these opportunities, and I quickly became adept at identifying different family networks. High-quality preparation was essential for all of these events, spending lots of time with individuals beforehand, and it was clear that this was time well spent. I would have liked to be able to spend more time following up pastoral offices afterwards, but rarely had the space in my diary to give this the emphasis I would have liked.

For thy Church that evermore
lifteth holy hands above,
offering up on every shore
this pure sacrifice of love:
*Lord of all, to thee we raise
this our sacrifice of praise.*

14

Liz Palin

————•◆•————

Liz is a full-time stipendiary curate in a team ministry in Cheltenham. But that hasn't – since ordination – always been the case! When she was ordained in 2011 she was director of Glenfall House (Gloucester Diocese's retreat house) and a self-supporting minister. She trained for ordination at WEMTC at the same time as studying for her MA in applied theology at The Queen's Foundation in Birmingham. Prior to ordination and since leaving university 28 years ago, Liz has worked in a variety of diocesan retreat houses. Her current curacy includes a varied mixture of traditions, though predominantly Anglo-Catholic.

* * *

Has anything really changed?

I vividly remember walking into the office in Glenfall House, the day after my ordination, and thinking to myself, 'Has anything really changed?' Of course much had changed. I was now ordained! I could wear a dog collar and I had a licence to minister as an Anglican deacon. I had taken on public life and people would see me differently. There was much to learn and a whole new world of ordained ministry ahead of me. Yet at the same time, much on that first day felt very familiar as I continued to live (with my family) and work at Glenfall House. I remember that I had a business committee meeting first thing, then a retreat house supporters' social event in the evening. In and among that was the usual round of things to sort out: staffing issues, guests' queries, and all the tasks associated with being a director of the retreat house.

During the day a fellow newly ordained curate phoned me – she was full-time stipendiary and had been asked to visit a parishioner in hospital. The phone conversation went something like this: 'I've been asked to go and see this person, they won't know who I am, what am I supposed to do?' I replied, 'You walk into the ward, say hello, my name is so-and-so and I'm the new curate. How are you?' I put the phone down, and reflected on our two very different first days as ordained ministers. I wasn't due to do anything in the parish until the following weekend, apart from a walk through of some liturgy on the Thursday.

It struck me that despite all the talk of 'doing church' differently, of fresh expressions, of intentional communities, to name but a few, I was still stuck in the mindset that if you weren't a full-time curate in a traditional parish setting, you were somehow not doing ministry properly. Much of the conversation about ministry during training had focused on the parish context, which I think had led me – at least in part – to feel that way. It also felt as though, for other curates, the immense experience of the moment of ordination in the cathedral was translated into a completely new way of 'being' and 'doing', but for me it felt like business as usual. I spent some time reflecting on this and part of me also wondered if God might be calling me at some stage to full-time parish ministry.

In the meantime, and being newly ordained, I set to with my various responsibilities. It was bit of a juggling act, what with work at the retreat house, parish duties, the curate training programme and family life, but I managed – somehow – and very definitely learned as I went along. It can be challenging to achieve a good balance when there are various demands on our time, but I have found that being reminded of the need to establish good boundaries helps, as does the ability to realize our own limitations (we can't do absolutely everything!). Accepting that, for me, is an ongoing challenge.

Meanwhile, clouds were gathering in respect of the future of Glenfall House. Major decisions needed to be made about the long-term financial viability of the retreat house. The recession had taken its toll and we could not continue to function without some injection of capital, but every avenue that was explored proved to be unfruitful. Things were not looking good and my future was far from certain. What would happen to me, to my colleagues, to our family, to my curacy, to those for whom the retreat house was their 'church'?

It was a particularly unsettling time. I tried to focus on reminding myself that God *had* called me to ordained ministry, and would not abandon me, but at times it was – if I am honest – incredibly challenging. Being part of a small team where you live and work can be wonderful, but exercising leadership of that team in difficult circumstances such as these was hard. In particular, there was the question of balancing personal friendships, pastoral relationships and confidential business information. I felt pulled in several directions and there were times when I wasn't sure what to say or do. Relationships with a range of people and organizations became strained, and loyalties became blurred. I was caught up in the middle of trying to be loyal to my staff, loyal to my employers and loyal to my bishop and senior clergy, when at times they seemed – at least to me – to be on opposing sides with differing priorities. Knowing on which occasions to keep my head below the parapet proved a steep learning curve!

Amid all this turmoil there was one thing of which I was absolutely sure. It would be crucial for me to find ways to be fed and sustained spiritually. We are told during training and selection that this is important, but it is quite a different matter when we are in a difficult situation and *actually* need to find a way to connect with God. But it is vital in ordained life, and indeed in the Christian life, to keep ourselves 'spiritually buoyant' because there will be tough times. We are not – unfortunately – promised an easy ride just because we follow Christ. For me, it was a time when I rediscovered the wonderful way in which the discipline and rhythm of the daily office and the Eucharist are a 'spiritual harbour' to take refuge in amid the storm.

The daily office with its familiar canticles, psalms and Scripture readings offered for me lament and joy, suffering and freedom and kept me going when I was too bruised and battered to pray much at all. This is one of the great strengths of the daily office and indeed of liturgy. It is 'there', available and offered for us when at times finding words to pray or to express or explore faith might be too difficult. I found the liturgy of the daily office to be a real gift in this time. And, of course, the discipline (and charge for all clergy!) of saying morning and evening prayer every day was helpful because it meant that I *would* sit down to pray and read the Bible daily.

It was also the Eucharist that fed me spiritually during this time, and my reflection is that since being 'priested', presiding at the Eucharist has been without doubt a key part of my priestly ministry. Having worked for 28 years offering God's generous welcome to all who come through the doors of a retreat house, to stand in the chapel of Glenfall House and preside at the Eucharist was an incredibly powerful moment for me. 'Why?' you might ask. My experience of presiding in that context was of being a channel of God's grace at the meal of all meals. And in the parish in which I celebrated my first Eucharist as a priest, I was the first woman to preside at the parish Eucharist in that church, a church that has been there for hundreds of years. It was quite an occasion and I was very aware of its significance. I felt as though, standing there, calling on the Holy Spirit to transform the bread and wine, and those who partook of it, that I was standing at a point in history. It was a very special moment as I placed the sacrament in the outstretched hands of those who had been on a long journey, one that had led them to a place where they were accepting women's priestly ministry for the first time.

All change!

I remember the occasion, standing in a churchyard about to begin guiding some local schoolchildren through an Easter story experience. It was then that I received the phone call telling me that a decision about the future of Glenfall House had been agreed. It was to close. I had been expecting the news but it still came as a shock to me.

I hardly had time to process the news before I was walking 260 schoolchildren through the Last Supper, the betrayal, the crucifixion and resurrection! It seemed, however, both right and in a sense ironic to be reflecting on those powerful themes at that particular time. I was also acutely aware that there was for me a sense of relief because a significant period of uncertainty, with all of the difficulties and challenges that had come with it, was now over. A decision had been made. The situation was out of my control and I had somehow to look to the future with my family.

The time leading up to the closure of Glenfall House was fairly short. It was a time when I gained a great deal of experience in managing change and public representative ministry. For example, I became a focus for people's anger (fellow clergy tell me this is not uncommon – be warned!) and I witnessed and ministered to people's pain and hurt. I came to accept that the decision to close the retreat house was not a personal reflection on my ministry. It was not actually about me, even though, of course, it affected me and my family in a personal way. I learned a bit about 'taking things on the chin' when necessary. Not an easy lesson, I have to say, but still it was part of my experience. I learned a lot about grace and humility.

Twenty-eight years of retreat house ministry, mostly lay but in recent months priestly, was coming to an end at an alarming rate of knots. My curacy was going in a direction I never thought it would take. I think back to that first day as a curate when I asked myself, 'Has anything really changed?' The obvious answer at this point would be, 'My goodness, and how!' The situation at times did feel out of control, but when we are faced with change and uncertainty it may be helpful to remind ourselves of certainties and constants. It can help to root us and be a stabilizing influence. I remember saying to myself that I am still the person God called into priestly ministry. I am still the person who has a sense of humour that allows me to smile in the midst of it all, the person who believes in life in all its fullness, the person who now more than ever wants to join in with God to see signs of the kingdom in new ways and places. Even in the mess and muddle of it all we can still be sure of who we are and our calling, but sometimes we need to take a step back and remind ourselves of this. I was also blessed with a training incumbent who was incredibly supportive throughout my curacy, with a husband who put up with my uncertainty and doubt, and with children who put up with my mood swings – even if at times, because of confidentiality, I couldn't explain why. Those people were a stabilizing and affirming influence in it all.

New beginnings

I was fortunate (or was it providential? Discuss!) that a way was found for me to complete my curacy. There is no doubt that the bishop was key in this being sorted out. I am now a full-time stipendiary curate in a parish. As I reflect back on my curacy story and my initial feeling that full-time parish ministry might be for me, I have to say that I am not sure this is how God had intended it to happen. I recall sitting with my bishop reflecting with him on this point. My theology tells me (and I believe it is sound theology) that God did not allow the closure of Glenfall House just so that I had to finally listen and respond to the call to full-time parish ministry. I don't think he works in that way but – vitally and reassuringly – he is there in the midst of our humanity, with all of its faults and mess. And I do believe in a God of redemption and new life. Whatever the situation, the Christian gospel offers us hope in something better to come. It is a forward-looking faith.

Being a curate has taught me that God's call on our lives doesn't stop when we are selected for training (which feels such a huge step), or when we are ordained. Calling is not in this sense a one-off event, so that we are called and then it stops. That's just not the way it works. Not in my experience anyway. God keeps on calling us to follow him. Sometimes it seems as if God is way ahead of us and we can't (or don't want to) catch up with him. Sometimes God is alongside us, an arm around the shoulder, walking alongside us, helping us make the journey. And sometimes God is holding us, letting us abide in his love and teaching us to trust him. The trick, I think, is to learn to hear God's calling in our lives despite the noise and confusion of life's circumstances, and then to faithfully respond. So, in each day, we might ask ourselves in prayer – what is God calling me to do and be today?

The sending out at the end of the ordination service begins with the words 'God who called you is faithful'. I remember it as one of the most spine-tingling parts of the service, delivered with such conviction and hope by the bishop. Throughout the many changes being a curate has brought me, those words echo again and again. It's true – God who calls you *is* faithful.

Part 4

WHAT MAKES
A GOOD CURATE AND
A SUCCESSFUL CURACY?

15

Paul Butler

———•◆•———

Paul Butler is the Bishop of Durham. He was converted as a teenager and his call to full-time ministry came at the same time. He spent six years in Nottingham as a student, a social work assistant and a travelling secretary for the Universities and Colleges Christian Fellowship. He trained for ordination at Wycliffe Hall, Oxford, during which time he married Rosemary. His ordained ministry has seen him serve as a curate in Wandsworth, an evangelist and manager with Scripture Union, a non-stipendiary minister, Team Rector of Walthamstow, and an area dean. In 2004 he was shocked to be called to be a bishop. His episcopal years have seen him serve as Bishop of Southampton, Southwell and Nottingham, and now Durham. He is also a canon of Byumba in Rwanda. Paul and Rosemary have four adult children. Paul is a writer, former chair of the Church Missionary Society and president of Scripture Union. He is passionate about the Church, especially children within it and its worldwide reality.

* * *

It was my deep privilege to conduct and preach at the funeral of my training incumbent, the Revd Allan Sirman, in the autumn of 2012. I felt honoured that after the many years that had passed since we ministered together, Allan asked that I, of all those with whom he had ministered, should take this special service. I am acutely aware that my own experience of being a curate in Wandsworth, with Allan and the wonderful people of the parish of All Saints with Holy Trinity, has been formative for my whole ministry in a range of ways. I had a long history of lay preaching and worship leading so was confident in these disciplines already. Nevertheless learning to preach more regularly, at a range of services and into a largely working-class and multi-ethnic setting, soon taught me that learning these disciplines is actually a lifelong task. It's one to which I remain deeply committed.

Learning the opportunities and skills in handling all that goes with the occasional offices was an unexpected joy. Standing outside Holy Trinity greeting Richie Benaud and the Bedser twins, along with a host of other cricketing greats, after conducting Jim Laker's funeral with Allan was both daunting and a thrill. It also helped me realize that everyone has the same sadness and needs when a friend dies. Fame and fortune do not change this. Such occasions could also be very humorous; the great horror star Vincent Price reading at his producer's funeral had everyone smiling alongside their sadness. Naturally most occasional offices were with the 'ordinary' people of the parish, but these were no less significant. Steph and Harm came to get married. At the time, the remarrying of a divorcee was rare and we offered a service of blessing after a civil marriage; the huge smile on both their faces that this was possible still lives with me. Their happiness on the day was evident to all. Steph became a regular worshipper and has continued in leadership elsewhere in her local congregation to this day. Positive pastoral contact at a point of need has led to a lifetime of Christian service.

What I learned most, in all aspects of my curacy, was the importance of relationships. First is the critical importance, for my own walk as a disciple of Jesus, and for the ordained ministry to which I have been called, of my relationship with God himself. Daily prayer and time in the Scriptures and times away for longer reflection were all learned during these first years. Patterns have changed over the years with the changing nature of family life and ministry context, but the fundamental necessity of this ongoing relationship with the Lord himself has been and remains foundational.

Second is the importance of relationships in the parish. Building strong relationships with regular worshippers is important. Equally so are the relationships with people in the community who may never come near church but for whom I hold a responsibility ('the cure of souls'). It is also essential to create key relationships with the gatekeepers in the community; these include politicians, civil servants, head teachers and community leaders. It is worth investing heavily in building strong working relationships and friendships with such people. Sandy was a regular in the local community centre, where many dropped in for coffee. The estate was full of rough diamonds; Sandy was gentler. The friendship built through simply dropping by regularly meant that when a crisis in her family life arose it was me that she turned to for advice and support. For Sandy this led to faith in Jesus Christ and a changed life.

Third is the value of relationships with fellow leaders in the church. In my curacy this was learning about teamwork with the incumbent, a youth worker, a London City Missioner and a senior curate. It was equally about readers, children's work leaders, home group leaders, PCC members, and music or worship leaders. All of these relationships matter. They all need time, and if invested in will bear fruit. My natural style is collaborative, but even so I was amazed at just how many relationships needed to be built here. I failed in very many ways; and believe I learned through those failures.

This was my final key lesson from my curacy: learn from your mistakes. Failure is not the end. It is a learning opportunity, a springboard for growth and a better future ministry. I am grateful that Allan allowed me to experiment and make mistakes; I would not be the bishop I am now without this.

Being a training incumbent

In Walthamstow it was my privilege to train three curates and see a number of people develop and train as readers and for ordained ministry. It is hard work because it means investing serious time, energy, prayer and emotion into helping a colleague grow and develop as the person God wants her to be, not create a clone of myself. It is so easy to try and make the person do it the same way that you do yourself, when the vital thing is that she should learn how to be herself from the experience, encouragement, and occasional rebuke that you as the trainer give. My three colleagues were very different people, temperamentally, spiritually, in age and experience. I served alongside two men and one woman in this role.

Dave and I shared an amazing two weeks in Byumba, Rwanda leading training sessions for all the clergy. Dave has very conservative eating habits and had never visited an African nation before. We shared laughter over his ability to handle the very different diet. We enjoyed great banter with Samuel and Elson, our two interpreters, as we kept using English idioms that had no obvious Kinyarwandan parallels. At the end of the visit we talked about Dave's future. I had gone on the trip having been invited to become Bishop of Southampton; after talking about his future Dave turned to me and said, 'What about yours? I hope they make you a bishop.' I could have fallen through the floor. But later, when I told him I was moving to become a bishop, he reminded me of the conversation, saying, 'You are a better liar than I thought; you never flinched in Byumba when I talked with you.' Curates offer perceptive, if sometimes painful, insights into their training incumbents' gifts and character.

I am deeply aware that I learned as I went on. I have little doubt that Dave, as the third curate, gained more from me than Jeremy or Rosie, although I think they too learned something from our work together. I was aware from the outset that this role is never one-way. I learned much from all three; from their own wisdom and experience; from their willingness to ask hard questions and attempt different things. I was glad of their critique of me, though perhaps did not tell them so often enough. Increasingly, though, I was aware of the team nature of how curates grow and learn. The input of other ordained colleagues (a definite plus of being in a team ministry!) was a further dimension. So too was the encouragement and advice that came from churchwardens, readers and members of the parish. All played their part in helping Jeremy, Rosie and Dave learn and be formed into Christlikeness. To adapt a phrase, 'It takes a church and community to train a curate'.

My overriding memory is that training curates was fun. I loved working with all three of these remarkably gifted people.

And so to being a bishop

The discerning of people's vocation is one of the greatest responsibilities and joys given to me as a bishop. Incumbents, vocations advisers, DDOs and both diocesan and National Panel members are all involved in the process, but at the end of the day it is my decision as bishop to endorse someone for training. Then, with advice, I choose to ordain that person. Part of this process is the careful discernment of where each person should serve their training post as a curate (or 'title', a term that after all this time I still find strange). So for what do I look in this part of an ordained minister's formation?

Relationship is key

Do I, along with others, think that this person will develop a good relationship with this particular training incumbent, and with the parish(es) in which he or she serves? The relationship with the incumbent is crucial but it does not stand alone. There should be other key guiding figures around the curate: a spiritual director (or soul friend), possibly an external supervisor, and the initial ministerial trainer – all play an invaluable role. So too do all the people of the parish, those outside and inside the Church. The curate will grow through building all these relationships, so placing him or her somewhere where it looks as though these will work matters.

Tom was rather taken aback when it was initially suggested that he serve in a town context; he thought a poor patch in a city would suit him best. However, he found in his training incumbent a companion who recognized his past ministry and set him free to engage in the local community in unexpected ways. He so valued being asked to serve as a school governor that he is now passionate about education and education policy. He looks back and sees the wisdom of putting him in a place of some surprise and discomfort, for it was one that stretched him in new ways. He highlights that the relationship with his incumbent was the most formative factor of all.

Context matters

A curacy is the setting for exercising ordained ministry for the first time, and therefore for learning a great deal about how the person functions best with his or her gifts and calling. Real growth only happens, then, in contexts that will not always be comfortable. Some stretching of experience is essential for real development – yet it must not be so much of a stretch that it breaks the person. So weighing up the churchmanship, style, social setting, support for family, etc., can be a tough balancing act. Some discomfort, I believe, makes for a better training context; but too much leads to potential long-term damage. Overall not enough people are training in rural, inner-city or outer estate contexts. For too many curates a suburban middle-class training sits too comfortably with their background. There is also a failure to train enough people away from the south and south-east of England.

The importance of context means that gaining experience in different contexts through the period of a curacy is vital. Spending some time in a different parish, in terms of both churchmanship and social context, is very helpful. I believe that every curate should gain experience, too, in at least one area of sector ministry by spending regular time in a hospital, prison or armed forces unit, etc. This broadens the overall learning. Phoebe, a self-supporting minister, initially became interested in hospital ministry through visiting parishioners. Her interest led to her asking to undertake a placement in a local hospital, where the chaplaincy team recognized her gifts. Here she found the heart of her ministry and she is now engaged in it as her primary focus.

I am also committed to trying to ensure that every curate spends at least a couple of weeks in a different part of the world. This opens the person's eyes to the world Church, and helps him or her see mission in our own context very differently.

Peer learning

Alongside the parish context and relationships, the peer group is a key learning resource. Input from experts matters, and must be part of the training, but I remain convinced that for the peer group to openly compare their experience, and support and critique one another, is even more valuable. Making the space for this to happen in a variety of ways is essential. So I worry about any curate who opts out of learning from his or her peers. It tends to set a bad pattern for the person's long-term ministry. It militates against collaboration. It tends to mean a lack of commitment to lifelong learning.

Growing into Christ

What I look for most of all in every curate's training is that he or she is growing into Christ. It is appropriate that boxes are ticked to show that the person has gained different experiences of ministry and is competent in a wide range of ministries (and more than competent in some of them!). But what is vital is that there is a love for the Lord himself. I want to see ministers of the gospel growing into Christ-likeness in their life and ministry. I want them to be growing in their worshipping prayer life; in their knowledge of Scripture; and in their ability to teach it and apply it to life. I look for wisdom that comes from 'the fear of the Lord'. If this is not happening there is no way that lifelong learning and ministry will be sustained. Godly wisdom lies at the heart of ordained gospel ministry. At the end of the curacy, whether a person is going on to become an incumbent, a chaplain, an associate minister or focusing on ministry in the workplace, what he or she needs is to have grown into Christ more fully, and be passionate to keep growing into him, and lead others in the same direction.

Conclusion

Curacies can genuinely make or break a person's long-term ministry. A good curacy certainly establishes healthy patterns that serve the ordained minister well, long into his or her future. A good curacy also opens up fresh opportunities and gifts, as well as strengthening those that were already there. But what a good curacy does best is to form the minister into greater likeness to Jesus Christ.

16

Ruth Worsley

———◆•◆•———

Ruth is the Archdeacon of Wilts in the Diocese of Salisbury, which is mostly rural. She trained for ordination at St John's College, Nottingham and was ordained in 1996. Most of her ministry has been in urban settings in the Diocese of Southwell and Nottingham, as a parish priest, area dean and a member of the bishop's staff; and then in Southwark as Parish Development Adviser. She has served on General Synod, is a member of the national Vocations Strategy group to encourage a growth in minority ethnic vocations to ordination, and is a Queen's Chaplain.

* * *

I have had the great privilege of having three curate-in-training colleagues in the course of my priestly ministry, as well as having ordinands on placement and, as Dean of Women's Ministry, being involved in the ongoing support of curates in post. My own curacy and that of my colleagues all had a unique perspective, and that is the place to begin.

Our personal stories

My first curate, Celia, adopted two young children in the first year of her curacy; the second, Angela, broke her foot in the first month; and the third, Matthew, had profound physical disability and was wheelchair-bound. In my own case I stayed beyond curacy and became the priest-in-charge, with my training incumbent becoming my associate minister.

Our stories are part of who we are and thus need to be part of our ministry. I am not a believer in the view that you can or should keep your personal life separate from your ministry. That does not mean that you shouldn't establish personal boundaries and ensure that ministry does not become all-consuming! However, ordained ministry is a vocation, a way of life, rather than a professional job in the conventional sense.

Integral living

It was Celia's first week. As we drove out of the church community centre car park to visit a parishioner, we saw a group of adults, including a woman, kicking someone on the ground. It was an ugly scene but I felt we couldn't just drive past and so, armed only with dog collars, we stopped and challenged the group, who quickly dispersed. We took the injured man into the centre and offered to phone the police but he was reluctant for us to do this. When asked what we could do for him, he simply asked for a cigarette. We never discovered what the fight was about, but we knew that his attackers were not justified in trying to kill him. We made no judgements about him but simply stepped in to help. He was appreciative of our help in saving him from a threatening situation.

Our parish in Nottingham was a particularly challenging one and was considered to be one of the most deprived in the UK. The two female curates who served there with me were mothers, like me, and so had to think long and hard about bringing up their children in an area with such a tough reputation. The daily toll of burglaries, knife crime and drug abuse have a wearying effect on one's energy when one is already stretched by ministry to some of the most marginalized. However, it was also one of the most stimulating places in which to work.

One day an 18-year-old lad arrived at the centre very distressed. He had lost his parents and brother in a car accident and felt entirely alone. Over the years we knew him his life became worse: money he had inherited was spent on drugs and a descent into crime ensued. The opportunity of a new life in Canada with relatives was lost when he cashed in the ticket to feed his habit. He would seek us out when he was desperate for food and became abusive, threatened us with knives and stole from us when he didn't get the money he asked for. The personal cost of such ministry should not be underestimated. We recognized in dealing with this young man that ministry in such a context and with such fragile people is costly and reminds us of Christ's words to his disciples and any would-be follower: 'Whoever wants to be my disciple must deny themselves and take up their cross and follow me.'

However, the word 'sacrifice' seems to have been lost from the regular vocabulary of ministry in a society that tends to put greater store on seeking self-fulfilment. If we are to fulfil Christ's edict to 'make disciples' there needs to be some modelling of 'disciplining practices' in our own lives. Patterns of prayer, 'going the extra mile' and reaching out to the stranger were integral to the lives of my curates and meant that they have continued to choose for themselves stretching yet fulfilling places of ministry.

Open to learning

As a curate myself I was impressed by the way in which my training incumbent, Graham, was open to learning from others. During the first couple of years of my curacy, every six weeks or so, we would sit down for coffee with my husband, also ordained and in his first incumbency, to compare notes. Graham had only recently returned to the UK from a period of ministry within the Anglican Church in Pakistan and was very conscious of the differences he was discovering between the cultures. Learning together became a pattern for my training and their ministry.

It has struck me on several occasions that some curates see the moment of ordination as the point at which they can sign off on their training, when in fact the curacy itself is the 'hands-on' development of that training. I think I was fortunate in my curate colleagues in that the first two had both spent their final year with me on placement during their college pre-ordination training. It was not intended that they should remain with me post-ordination – in fact it was considered to be contrary to best practice – but as 'luck would have it' (perhaps God had a part to play in it!), they ended up with me as their training incumbent. Their entry to curacy was thus something of an extension to the learning process begun in college. This contributed to their being open to continual learning and established a pattern for their future ministerial development.

One of my concerns has been that ordination training has sometimes not helped in developing this way of living and learning, because it often dismisses or ignores the transferable skills that people bring with them into such learning environments. Ordinands can feel deskilled, feel that their previous life has no relevance to their current experience. As a result you find some students wanting to assert their right of exemption from certain areas of study without appreciating the contribution they in turn make to the learning of others. I believe this can seriously undermine the concept that we are all participants in a learning journey alongside others throughout our ministry.

We had a very structured system of evaluation within curate training, which meant that reflective practice was a frequent and regular part of my working with each of my curate colleagues. I don't know how much they learned, but I certainly learned from them! That mutual commitment was a strong base for our working relationship.

Boundaries, loyalty, friendship?

Angela took great care over her first funeral and spent time visiting the young woman who had lost the mum she adored. This led the woman to become a regular attender at church and discover faith for herself. It also, however, led to an unhealthy dependence upon and transference of her adoration to the curate.

The development of relationship is an essential part of ministry, and modelling it in our professional roles is therefore important. I am not of the view that clergy cannot have friends within their parishes. How we manage the boundaries and conflicts of confidentiality, though, is part of the learning process.

A promise I made to my training incumbent on arrival, and one I looked for from my curate colleagues, was that we would maintain our loyalty to one another whatever the circumstances we faced and whether or not we disagreed. This was not a blind loyalty that required unanimity of views. We would commit to being open and honest with each other and argue our case in the privacy of our one-to-one conversations and meetings. Once a decision was reached, however, it was clear that we would each support the other in the direction decided upon. We presented a united front in PCC meetings or when required to give a lead. This didn't mean that there was no room for debate or discussion, to which we each contributed, but it did mean that we didn't leave room for the undermining of the other.

I recall in my first year of curacy that someone in a consultancy role made some flattering remarks about the difference my arrival had made within the parish. Indeed, I was flattered, but the implication also being made in this instance was that the maker of those remarks didn't think much of my training incumbent. As a result I felt the need to draw some boundaries that made it clear that I did not see my position as one that would in any way conflict with that of my clergy colleague.

I think that sometimes there is a tendency for both curate and training incumbent to assume that friendship will be a natural outcome of their working relationship. I've found that in each of my own relationships with a curate or training colleague there has been a deep sense of appreciation, sharing of a very personal nature, and trust that has developed between us. Indeed a friendship. However, this hasn't automatically transmuted into lifelong commitment, sharing in lots of social occasions, or finding our families become best buddies.

Collaboration not individualism

My back would ache standing at the dining-room table that took the place of an altar in one church; but it was just the right height for Matthew in his wheelchair. I would stand alongside him as he spoke the words of consecration and would elevate the bread and wine, being his hands. As we moved from person to person he would bless and I would sign with the cross. This was the broken body of Christ in sharp reality. His cheerful acceptance of his own vulnerability and need of others was the greatest lesson of all.

Making the most of such moments requires wisdom and insight. How do we allow our vulnerability to show through and speak spiritual truths into people's hearts and minds without this becoming an exhibition of our own insecurities, or an emotive discharge? Clergy who have learnt to share their personal stories, faults and failings in ways that contribute to the growth of understanding for others' spiritual journeys have learnt wisdom indeed.

The blessing I have received through working with my curate colleagues has been immense, and our journey together as ordained ministers underlines the value of collaboration. We have, collectively, recognized God's calling to us all to ministry together, telling the story of God's love.

17

Sue Hemsley-Halls

———•◦•———

Sue is a vocations adviser and DDO for the Diocese of Southwell and Nottingham. Prior to ordination, she was a special needs teacher working first in special schools and later as coordinator of a communication project. She trained for ordination at Cranmer Hall and was ordained in Lichfield Cathedral in 1995. Her ministry experience includes being a curate in a former mining area, vicar in a professional suburban area and chaplain to deaf people.

* * *

In a section entitled 'What makes a good curate and a successful curacy?', you might expect to find a series of anecdotes about flourishing curacies designed to encourage and inspire those on the path towards ordination, and tales of curacy disasters to warn the unwary. Yet the role of a DDO involves not so much story-telling but rather active listening. The DDO or vocations adviser is someone who walks beside the ordination enquirer on her vocational journey, hearing her story, helping her to articulate those inner stirrings and God-given nudges. The DDO hopefully brings new insights, and makes suggestions about the best path to take when crossroads are reached, particularly regarding a choice of training college or course, and setting up a curacy.

Most DDOs would have sufficient material to write a book about candidates they have known. People's life and faith stories include elements that may be funny, shameful, inspiring, faithful, shocking, illegal, doubtful or redemptive, so trust and appropriate confidentiality are required by the listener. I am therefore leaving it to others to tell their own stories, and am focusing on the 'background story' of how matching ordinands to curacies comes about.

As an active listener throughout the discernment process and train-ing, the DDO needs to be realistic and informed about the candidate. As Bishops' Advisory Panels are booked, DDOs must honestly present candidates with their unique personalities, strengths, hang-ups and weaknesses, and any complications from the past or present. They have to avoid simply trying to get them through the system, no matter how genuine their calling seems to be or how likeable they are. Matching ordinands to curacies involves the same objective, informed judgement. So a successful curacy starts right back with the discernment process. The criteria for selection require the candidate's vocation to be realistic, obedient and informed. People need to be aware of what they are being called to, with the clarity to see the Church both as it is today, and also as it is likely to develop over the next few decades. Sometimes people seeking curacies seem to have a fixed image of an ideal church where they wish to serve, then wonder why they can't find the post that they are looking for. Ordinands' expectations may be based on positive experience of their home parish from an earlier stage in life, or their sending church. It is to be hoped that initial training helps develop their horizons and gives them increased confidence to step out into new situations in ministry.

During the discernment process, it is important for the DDO to visit candidates in their homes and understand their home situation, because when someone is ordained, especially in a full-time stipendiary role, their whole family is involved. Wise decisions are needed regarding training options, and whether the family move or stay in their own home at this point. Curates who receive a stipend are nationally deployable, and people must take this seriously at an early stage, not wait until the first curacy offers are made before they face the reality about whether they and their family feel able to relocate.

Timing is essential. An enquirer with huge potential may come forward but discussion may be needed about whether it's the right time, especially if the person concerned has a family. Moreover, it is not only our human concept of good timing but, crucially, God's timing that needs to be considered. I know an ordinand who had a strong sense of calling to ordained ministry, but year after year, for various reasons, he made little progress on the path to ordination. Yet the strong sense of calling did not weaken and he was enlightened about God's timing by reflecting on the story of David. When David was anointed by the prophet Samuel as a sign of being called by God, he was not required to take up his task from that particular day but returned to look after the sheep before becoming one of the most significant figures in the history of Israel.

Looking towards the end of training, some people reach a point where they wish to be challenged further. Their training experiences have acted as a catalyst for their desire to encounter more challenges and to continue to broaden their understanding and push the boundaries. Others may feel that training has already taken them beyond their comfort zone and they now want to stay within a tradition or social situation that they are comfortable with.

A curacy is the first, exciting phase of a new ministry and it sets the foundation for future ministry. The experiences in a curacy, both good and bad – the practice and development of ministerial skills, the reflection on events and situations, and the challenges that are faced – all have a long-term impact. Key to all this is the curate's relationship with the training incumbent, and my role includes helping to discern who would be a good training incumbent.

This diocese doesn't simply match curates with a training incumbent because there's always been a curate in that particular parish. Members of the First Appointments Team – the two archdeacons, the Director of Ministry and Mission, the Ministry Development Adviser, the Dean of Women's Ministry and myself, all help discern the best training opportunities for a curate. With regard to training incumbents, we look for someone with a good background in ministry, but also someone who is collaborative and would have a good working relationship with a curate. We consider as well whether the parish is a good learning context, but the potential relationship with the training incumbent is vital. Sometimes experienced training incumbents are asked to take on the role, but we also ask others who may have less experience but in whom we see the ability to train, to relate well to others, and to be good role models.

One way of extending the pool of training incumbents in this diocese has been to offer enquiry days for potential training incumbents, enabling them to think through the role more fully. These include group exercises that explore specific scenarios about how the participants would deal with difficult situations, and reflecting on their priorities in curate training.

Our First Appointments Team considers how best to match potential curates with training incumbents from an agreed shortlist. In the matching process it's usually the DDO who knows the ordinands best, while the other members of the First Appointments Team will probably know the church or the training incumbent much better than they know the curate. Our recommendations regarding matches are communicated to the bishop, who makes the final decision.

However, we all know that human beings are unpredictable and what seems a good match initially may, once the curate is in post, not work out – and it is not usually all one person's fault! When people work closely together, issues emerge and getting a match that will endure and be positive for everyone involved can be challenging. Neither family relationships nor the parish relationship can be fully predicted, but both need to be borne in mind when placing a curate. These and other relationships affect how the curacy develops. For example, the impact of having a new curate as a member of the leadership team can affect the existing relationship dynamic, and it could be a threat for some established members of the team.

People's individual needs and former experience are considered by the First Appointments Team, but potential curates should not expect that all their needs and preferences will be met. An element of sacrifice may be involved. It is important to try to project the learning and development needed by the individual during his or her curacy but also to encourage the curate to be open to new insights. Willingness to learn is needed on both sides. Opposites can often work quite well together. I know of one person who didn't think a curacy would be a good match because she and the vicar were too alike. It would have been unlikely to fail as a curacy, but there might not have been the creative dynamic that other combinations can have.

Training incumbents should respect the ability and gifts of the curate and be secure enough in themselves to allow and appreciate that the curate may have greater skills in some areas. It's important for both to be team players − and if the curate is not a collaborative person when starting his or her curacy, then this is something he or she will need to learn. Respect and trust on both sides are crucial. The training incumbent should sometimes be willing to take some considered risks: we can always be surprised by what someone else's input or different approach can achieve. Curates should be ready to take on board the advice and experience of the trainer.

The DDO's role includes ensuring that the working agreement is clear and mutually acceptable to all parties, especially when someone is working part time, in a pioneering context, or where arrangements regarding childcare are needed. Curate and trainer need to talk things through in advance and have an understanding of how problems can be sorted out if their circumstances or needs change. The working agreement should include something about later negotiations if one of the parties isn't happy. It is important that curates are aware of the proper processes to follow if they encounter problems. If difficulties can't be resolved even though process is followed properly, the pain can be minimized. Both curate and trainer need to be supported when things go wrong, since any sense of failure is usually felt by all. There should be no private or public apportioning of blame.

When seeking a curacy, I would like to encourage ordinands to focus first and foremost on how they can serve, rather than on their own personal needs or their own development. Of course, these things are important, but our calling is to share in God's work among God's people in every place and every situation. Taking the important decision of where to serve a title post can be a stressful and confusing process, but God who has called us will also be with us as we go.

18

Tom Barron

————•◦•◦•————

Tom has been married to Sonia for 23 years; she has been a curate for the past two and a half. He is a solicitor in private practice, and likes reading and spiders. The reflection that follows is drawn mostly from his own experience, but as this is the only chapter in the book written by a curate's spouse he has taken the opportunity to consult with a few others, whose help is gratefully acknowledged. You know who you are!

* * *

If it is hard to generalize about the characteristics of curates nowadays, it is harder to generalize about their spouses. Nothing is typical. Some, still, are young mothers. Some are housewives or househusbands. Not a few have professional qualifications and careers. Some have barely finished writing thank-yous for wedding presents; others have been married for decades. Some have plenty of time available to contribute to the life of the church; others much less. I have found most curates' spouses fairly intelligent, but even that is not quite universal. (If you are a curate's spouse reading this, you are one of the intelligent ones.)

In the early days it was strange to think of my wife as an ordained minister of the Church, endowed by her bishop with an authority that neither I nor the rest of the family shared in (believe it or not, she promised to obey me when we married); and strange, too, to receive communion from her. A curate's authority is, in fact, rather a curious thing altogether. From the point of view of non-churchgoers, or very irregular attenders, a curate is the vicar's number two; an anointed representative of the Church of England and even of God. To the chosen flock, a curate is a mere trainee, a passing, ephemeral insertion into the intricate fabric of church dynamics, which in three years' time will close over the space where she has been.

Since Sonia received and acted upon her call to ordained ministry, our family has got off pretty lightly. The sacrifices have hardly been worthy of the name. Sonia had an interview for a curacy at a church in an urban priority area and we were all set for the challenge of living and working there; but the vicar and wardens didn't feel that we were called to them. We ended up at a well-resourced, broadly evangelical church in an affluent suburb, almost regrettably similar – as we would have liked to broaden our experience – to some that we had formerly attended. We have had to move to a somewhat smaller house, and it takes me a little longer to drive to work than before. Perhaps the drawback that we felt most keenly was that our younger son did not like inviting his friends to the new house; but he was well into his teens and at least could stay at the same school. Overall, God could hardly have asked less of us.

Other curates' spouses – especially where there are young children involved – are called to make more drastic changes. One of my contacts has exchanged his full-time work for part-time, and this is not unusual. He is earning less, the management found it hard to understand, and in his line there are not so many part-time jobs available. But he also reports significant compensations; less necessity for after-school clubs for the children, less pressure to work overtime, more time to get on top of the housework and support the Church's ministry.

In my case, Sonia had already been working in a fairly high-pressure job, and while being a curate has been no less demanding for her, the new work has not resulted in our seeing less of each other than before. The nature of our mutual support has, however, undergone certain changes. We no longer have the same day off and it is difficult to get away as a family, or even as a couple. The people of the parish have legitimate claims on Sonia and on her time, and I am conscious of the need to share her with them. I almost always cook lunch on Sundays (visitors usually don't realize this and Sonia graciously receives the compliments on my behalf), and sometimes, which is more challenging, I even have to *plan* what the lunch is going to be beforehand. The curate's sermons are usually practised on me before they are allowed to see the light of day; and naturally the worse the sermon, the more often I have to listen to it before it is ready to be unleashed.

Of course, emergencies will arise in the church from time to time. A meeting will be due to start in 15 minutes, and umpteen tables and six times umpteen chairs have to be set up; and her husband naturally becomes the first port of call the harassed curate turns to for help. Sometimes the spouse's extra work is planned in advance. Last autumn Sonia was the UK organizer for a two-week visit by a group of 16 Canadians who had come to give Christian dramatic performances in various parts of the country, on a very limited budget. The logistical challenges, and the extent to which your author was called upon to help meet them, may readily be imagined. But it was also one of the most rewarding projects I have taken part in, and a real privilege to befriend and serve a wonderful and very talented team.

Even today, it can be a difficulty for a curate's wife that the good people in your husband's church have preconceived notions about you, and especially about the sort of contributions you can make. At its worst, there can almost be an assumption that you are there to serve the church; that by paying for the services of a married male curate the Church of England is providing four hands instead of the usual two. If this happens, you may need to be very firm in stating where the boundaries lie. No one, however, expects the curate's *husband* to have a born enthusiasm for looking after babies or making cucumber sandwiches, or even, strangely enough, for basic DIY. I have received requests to be on the reading and coffee rotas, and latterly to be on the PCC, but I attribute this to routine talent-spotting rather than to any assumptions based on position.

These requests being in my judgement reasonable, I said yes each time. Incidentally I made a bad start on the PCC by promptly casting a vote which, as Sonia later explained to me, was for the wrong thing. Fortunately our relationship was strong enough to survive the fallout. (Quite easily, actually.)

Advice? If you don't have an outside occupation, there can be a danger of becoming subsumed in your spouse's identity. Do not let the Church dictate to you which activities you become involved in; choose them yourself, and you may have opportunities to explore your talents before your other half morphs into a vicar.

Sometimes you will have to act as a sounding board as the frustrations of the job are expressed. It goes without saying that a large part of your work here is to listen; a smaller part will be to offer detached advice. If it becomes apparent that particular individuals are a source of difficulty, keep it totally confidential. Occasionally you will see clearly that your spouse is acting unwisely; gently tell him or her so.

So far as lies within you, live peaceably with everyone. In fact I think this is something that most curates and indeed clergy spouses understand instinctively. In any church of moderate size, the curate has to contend with a fascinating mix of fallen humanity – opinionated senior citizens who tread where they've always trod, opinionated junior citizens whose zeal exceeds their judgement, opinionated silent types who are hurt when their unexpressed views aren't taken into account, followers of guidelines, ignorers of guidelines, dominant egos, fragile egos, and so on. (All lovely people, though.) Worse still, the curate isn't perfect either. In these circumstances, the last thing the curate needs is for his or her spouse to be identified with some *camp* within the church. While the curacy lasts, let Denis Thatcher, not Hillary Clinton, for all her admirable qualities, be your role model.

And – easily the most difficult for most of us, myself definitely included – do make time for each other. Here, having a full-time job is problematic because your day off will almost certainly be different from your spouse's, and he or she may not get many available evenings. It can be necessary to take the odd holiday at (from the point of view of your work) inconvenient times. But don't underestimate the importance of preserving your relationship with each other and with God. If that threefold cord doesn't get frayed, it will remain as it should be – not easily broken.

Part 5

THE RELATIONSHIP BETWEEN TRAINING INCUMBENT AND CURATE

19

Jonathan Perkin

—•◦•—

Jonathan is the vicar of St Andrew's Church, Churchdown, Gloucester. Prior to ordination, he taught geography at Ardingly College, West Sussex, from 1976 to 1987. He trained for ordination at Trinity College, Bristol, and was ordained in Exeter Cathedral in 1991. His first post was as curate of St Andrew's Church in Cullompton, Devon. He was then deputy rector in Ashtead, Surrey. His first incumbent's post was at St John's Church in Egham, Surrey from 2001 to 2005, where his first wife died suddenly in 2003. He married again in 2005, has six children, and moved to Gloucestershire in 2005 to take up his current post.

* * *

I always pray with joy because of your partnership in the gospel ...
(Philippians 1.4, 5)

It seems to me that the relationship between vicar and curate is second in importance after the relationship with one's spouse (if married, that is). At least, it feels like that at the time. It is close, intimate, vibrant, dynamic and fragile. I have been blessed with three great curates, all very different, and inherited two who luckily escaped me after a few months. My prayer is that they will have felt blessed by coming alongside my ministry and will have learnt something of the complexities of being a member of the clergy in the Church of England.

A lesson from Waitrose

The John Lewis Partnership is a visionary and successful way of doing business, boldly putting the happiness of Partners at the centre of everything it does. It's the embodiment of an ideal, the outcome of nearly a century of endeavour to create a different sort of company, owned by Partners dedicated to serving customers with flair and fairness.   (From the John Lewis website)

I like that. It speaks of what a good partnership is all about. Vision, success, happiness, endeavour, dedication, service, flair and fairness. Question: do those words sum up most curates' experience in their curacies? I fear the answer is, rarely.

I had an excellent curacy in Devon with a gifted vicar who, with humour and style, taught me a huge amount about ministry. At the age of 44, I felt prepared to move on with confidence. I then worked as a deputy rector in a large parish in Surrey. In a village setting, the rector had built a church that attracted over 1,200 every Sunday with worship styles ranging from Book of Common Prayer and sung Eucharist to all-age and charismatic contemporary services. Now that's the Church of England at its best. Encompassing every possible style of worship in eight services in one day. So I have experienced some great partnerships, although never without their challenges. Great leaders are sometimes tricky to negotiate, but they are still great leaders.

So, back to Waitrose. Another great quote is from its founder, John Spedan Lewis: 'The supreme purpose of the John Lewis Partnership is simply the happiness of its members.'

Ministry must be fun. That does not mean superficial or casual, and there will be very serious moments. But it must be fun. The happiness of my curate is key. There are too many morose, depressed and gloomy clergy around, looking like the TV's stereotypes. I want my curates to feel that they are having fun, even if ministry brings pressure, disappointment and heartache. I used to ask Mark, my curate in Egham, every Sunday in the vestry, 'Are we having fun yet?'

Mark was very fond of fun competitions. One summer he announced in church the 'Tallest Sunflower' competition. He gave me a sunflower seed, which I carefully planted, nurtured and watered for weeks. It never grew more than 18 inches, to my despair! After the competition was over, he then informed me that he had given me the dwarf variety.

Think of the great partnerships – Antony and Cleopatra, Victoria and Albert, Rudolf Nureyev and Margot Fonteyn, Marks and Spencer, Fortnum and Mason, Morecambe and Wise, Laurel and Hardy, Bonnie and Clyde, Butch Cassidy and the Sundance Kid. What is it that gives these partnerships such strength? The partners complement one another, combining their strengths and weaknesses. They compliment one another, with praise and encouragement. They share the same vision, can criticize each other's faults without defensiveness, and can create wholeness by rubbing bits off each other. They can defend each other from outside attack, while comforting one another in difficulty. If we can only focus on those attributes, then the partnership will be a happy one.

There may be 101 ways of describing the partnership between vicar and curate, but I want to focus on just three Rs: Respect, Relationship and Role modelling.

Respect

It is incredibly important for vicar and curate to respect one another. They will be different in so many ways – upbringing, background, education, experience, age, culture, spiritual maturity, ambition, etc. It is not surprising that such differences are likely to cause conflict in the partnership. I don't want my curate to become a mini-me, and yet deep down I might wish he was a little bit more like me because life is easier that way.

My present curate, Jon, turned up on his first Sunday for our traditional morning Communion service wearing a pair of blue denim jeans. At 25, why not? In the space of two minutes, I had to suppress my surprise, keep a cheery smile on my face and do a thorough cultural review in my head. Is this appropriate for the congregation, for him, for me, for God (who loves denim, I guess), for the future? Well, a couple of days later, after I had Googled 'CofE Dress Code/Fresh Expressions/Culture/Canons/twentysomethings', we had a gentle conversation about clothes.

The key is respect. I respect him even if he does things that I would not do, but respect him enough to talk through the issues. Now, I have never served with a woman curate. I don't know if I would ever be brave enough to comment on her dress. I leave that to those who have had women colleagues to advise.

Respect means acceptance, tolerance, admiration, forgiveness, affirmation, believing in and valuing the other. It also means loving the other person enough to confront, challenge, question, direct and suggest.

Relationship

Both parties must work on the relationship if it is to thrive. The question is, what kind of relationship? Of course, the relationship changes. Sometimes I may be the boss, the colleague, Dad, friend, mentor, coach or critic. At other times, I will need my curate's help, advice, sympathy, admonition or affirmation. I prefer to think of the relationship as a partnership, where I am the senior partner but where we have to work closely together if it is to succeed. The idea of bossing my curate around as if he were a junior clerk or of lower rank is frankly disgraceful. I don't see that in the relationship between the apostle Paul and Timothy (see 2 Timothy 1.1–7).

So, the relationship needs energy and imagination, and like all relationships will need working on. What you do will vary, but it might include the following. Make sure the larder is stocked with lovely goodies when the curate moves in. Presents for the spouse and children at Christmas.

Remember his or her birthday and those of the family. Take the couple out for a meal occasionally, and certainly invite them to Sunday lunch. Ordination gifts. Drop in with a bottle of wine to see the family are OK. Pick up on crises in the family. Provide meals when babies arrive, and even babysit – on one occasion my wife got up in the middle of the night to look after the other children while the curate took his pregnant wife into hospital. It all helps to cultivate a warm and loving relationship.

Make sure you know the wider family situation. On a professional level this might entail regular meetings outside staff meetings or daily offices, feedback sessions, planning sessions, away days, fun days, and times of just chewing the cud with no agenda at all. Well, I try anyway. All the training manuals will no doubt add to the list.

There will be moments of conflict in the relationship. Like all conflict situations, they need careful handling because it is vital to maintain the relationship. Differences in theological position are healthy but can cause friction. I remember a somewhat painful dialogue with one curate over what actually happens to the child at baptism. I am not sure we resolved the issue there and then, but we agreed to continue to think it through. It never raised its head again (the discussion, not the baby being baptized!). At least it meant we could respect each other while holding contrasting positions. Actually, the session on conflict in Holy Trinity, Brompton's 'Marriage Course' is as good as any in resolving the issues.

It seems to me that often conflict is more about me and my insecurities than about the curate. I hear too often stories of breakdown in the relationship between a vicar and curate because the vicar is threatened by the younger colleague, but the situation is presented to the church as a personality clash. In the words of James 3.10, 'My brothers and sisters, this should not be.' What I keep in my mind is that this curacy is going to affect the person concerned for the rest of his or her ministry. I want the curate to leave with good feelings and memories.

Role modelling

I am not just to respect my curate and develop the relationship; I must also be a good role model. It is very scary to think that the curate watches very closely how I pray, the words I use and the passion involved. He or she will emulate how I preach, observing the style, content, and faithfulness to Scripture and, even more nerve-racking, will notice how I speak of others in the congregation and how I relate to them. Perhaps most important of all, he will watch how I devote time to my wife and children. My whole Christian life is under the microscope in a way no one else (except my family) sees. That's both scary and a privilege. I want to share ministry, warts and all. I don't want there to be hypocrisy or posturing or pretending. This is what it is. I remember a well-known pastor saying that Christian ministry will make you either a better or a worse Christian. That's why my role modelling is so important. I want the curate to become the best he or she can ever be having been through my hands. A tall order, I know, but that's the ideal.

Another striking comment I came across the other day: 'Every organization starts with prophets but ends with policemen.' These curates come to us as prophets. They have vision, enthusiasm, perspective, energy and talent. The Church of England desperately needs them to retain that prophetic edge if it is to survive. So, we must be careful not to bash it out of them with rules and endless targets. Sure, they need to learn the skills but not so we can merely tick boxes. God save us from the 'target' culture which produces the right outcomes but with the wrong people.

So, thank you, Mark, Rob and Jon, for trusting yourselves to me. I have enjoyed working with you, I think you are amazing men of God, and I count it a privilege to have known you.

20

Alan Howe

———◆•◆•◆———

Alan is the vicar of Christ Church in Chilwell, Nottingham. Prior to ordination in 1980, he worked for the Greater London Council as a scientific officer (read lab assistant) on various aspects of environmental protection (read sewage). He has worked in a variety of parishes over 33 years and now serves in a large suburban parish in Nottingham. He has served as an area dean and as chair of the House of Clergy for the Southwell and Nottingham Diocese. He also conducts clergy development reviews and is involved in clergy training courses. He has trained four curates and supervised numerous ordinands on placement from St John's College, Nottingham.

* * *

Our diocese used to run a 'skills of supervision course' and the conductor brought two mildly humorous axioms that have stuck. First, he opined, 'The only thing worse than not having a curate is having one.' In spite of all the teaching to the contrary, there is the lurking feeling that getting a curate will bring a pair of hands to share the load. Parishioners say, 'You will be better off, now you have a curate.' They totally fail to note that training a curate is a job of work that demands the investment of quality time (in the early days a lot of time).

The second axiom was, 'Having a curate is like being married but without the sex.' It prompted a chuckle, but a good relationship between trainer and trainee is a very close one indeed. Looking through my phone and email logs, correspondence with the curate outstrips all other communications by a big factor and far outstrips the number of phone calls from my wife and family. When married couples make the promises they include 'poorer', 'worse' and 'sickness', and so can the training relationship. The more prepared both parties are for that, the better equipped they will be to know how to handle difficulties. With my current curate, we had two meetings to 'court' one another. The first meeting threw up questions, and these questions were presented and handled at a second meeting. It was easy for us because minimal travel was required, but I would say that even if it means a second tankful of petrol, some processing time is good. It might save hours of anguish in the future.

I have had a variety of experiences with curates in training, mostly good but with painful exceptions. In the stories that follow I hope to show the hard-won fruits of those experiences that span 20 years. For me two things have come to the fore: teachability and loyalty; and to misquote St Paul, the greatest of these is loyalty.

Curate A

I had just arrived in a new parish and a new diocese. The dust had not settled before an influential incumbent rang me up to soften the ground for a curate who was finishing training and whom the diocese was 'keen to keep'. First bit of advice to training incumbents: don't get pressured into it because the system is trying to solve a problem using you. Before I knew it, there was curacy candidate A in front of me and I was seeking to apply the criteria of Character, Competence and Chemistry that I had just learnt on a Willow Creek conference. Curate A was a nice chap, salt of the earth and all. I was a southerner; he was a local. The equation on offer was, 'You teach me how to "vicar" and I will teach you how to understand urban mining culture.'

I was keen to make my way in the diocese and sensed that saying 'yes' to this curate would notch up some points for me in the corridors of power. If I am truthful, however, there were lingering doubts in all three 'C' categories. I should have listened to them. Things were all right for a year in the training relationship, but in the church as a whole all was not well. A power group within the church who were deeply embedded in the mining culture found that they could relate well to Curate A but less well to me. I had mistakenly thought that being from a council estate background in London would help me understand working-class people in the mining town.

As the pressure grew, time that I knew I should be devoting to training got eaten up with fighting fires in the powerful leadership team. The pressures made home life difficult and one of our children began to truant from school. The message got back to me that the curate's family was unhappy with me. Then I was contacted by the training department, to be challenged on failing in my training responsibilities. The low point came when in an attempt to regain ground I invited A and spouse to a nice meal out which ended up in agonizing semi-silence and squirming embarrassment. There were several lessons to learn from that painful time:

1 Don't allow a trainer/trainee relationship to be forced in order to solve an external problem.
2 Do listen to the inner voice when it does not feel right, while there is still time to withdraw from the process.
3 Don't enter a training relationship because you feel it would be good for the parish.
4 Don't look to a curate to fill in the gaps in your own competences.
5 Do ask loyalty questions:
   (a) Will this person tell me when things are starting to go wrong?
   (b) Will this person watch my back and affirm me in an appropriate way?
   (c) Will this person trust me to affirm him/her in an appropriate way?
   (d) Do I trust this person?
6 Do ask teachability questions:
   (a) Will this person value my experience and feel he/she can learn from me?
   (b) Do I value this person's experience and feel that I can learn from him/her?
   (c) Will this person do what I ask, even when he/she personally would choose a different course?
   (d) Does this person respect me?

Curate B

This is a much more positive story but one that still contains some repeating elements. Curate B needed to be placed in the area because her husband was a priest. There were many more positive answers to the three 'C's and a much longer fuse on the difficulties. However, looking back at our first encounter I realize I was being interviewed by B rather than the other way round. I found myself anxious to give the right answers in order to close the deal, which was a win–win situation for me and the parish. The comments here are far more subtle because there is a right and a wrong way for curates to deepen their formation and become their own leader and their own person.

I look back to an outstanding training incumbent, but by the beginning of year three I was straining at the leash to go and do things more my own way. I sought to be loyal at each point but was finding loyalty harder as I realized that my incumbent's style and mine were quite different. He was a digger-in of heels whereas I am a compromiser. He asked me at one point to consider a fourth year but I realized that we could part as friends after three years with deep mutual respect, whereas the same might not be true after four.

With B the changes were subtle. Her attitude had been a joyful 'muck in with everything' for the first half of the curacy and it became a 'do what I'm asked' stance. The relationship never broke down and is still good, but it could have been so much better. B went on to explore theology and to handle big-picture issues. The feeling was that at a particular undefined point we drifted apart and respect was more grudgingly given. As this is essentially a partial success story, learning outcomes are fuzzy. I suspect that many curacies come under this heading and I have already indicated that my first curacy was one such. How, then, can one make what is good better? Here are a few thoughts:

1 Be clearer at the start. For example, if this is more of an arranged marriage than an ideal partnership of complementary minds, admit it and double check that you can both live with that.
2 Ask what it is that you most want to learn from me.
3 Ask what it is that I could learn from you.
4 Make a contract to speak up when items 2 or 3 above are perceived by either party not to be happening.
5 Have a very robust discussion in the middle of the curacy about what is going well and what frustrations exist.
6 Be honest with yourself as a trainer when you have not delivered on the contract. Don't 'pull rank' in an inappropriate way.

Curate C

In many cases nowadays, curates come with huge life experience from the top of their profession. I just want to mention one training relationship that went exceptionally well. Curate C had been a churchwarden in my parish and went forward for self-supporting ministry, and for deployment reasons served a curacy with me in his sending parish. This meant that I already knew him exceptionally well. He had been very gifted and able in his previous career and he knew it would be hard to be a (lowly) curate under a man younger than himself. We were able to talk freely about that and set some pretty firm guidelines as to how he would be a trainee, and these proved highly valuable as we worked together for three years. It is far from the norm, but in this ever-changing Church it may become increasingly hard to define normal.

Curate D

There is an excellent episode of the TV sitcom *Rev.* where the lovable but vulnerable parish priest, Adam Smallbone (Tom Hollander), has his world turned upside down by the arrival of Abi, an exceptionally talented curate. When Adam experiences Abi in action, he begins to doubt his own abilities and experience the age-old green monster of jealousy, with its sidekick self-doubt. OK, I put my hand up, I have been there with three of my four curates. With the arrival of Curate D, I had all a hard-working incumbent could wish for. D was mature and dripping with life experience. She had been a missionary with awesome tales of daring. She had been a secondary teacher managing her own department. She had worked for the national Church as a respected adviser in a pivotal role and, blow me down, in the middle of a talk to the men's fellowship, if she didn't whip out a guitar and start a self-accompanied song, playing and singing beautifully. 'It's just not fair, Lord!'

There was nothing for it but to make a public confession to my fellow training incumbents and director of training. Thankfully they had seen the episode of *Rev.* and knew where I was coming from. There were some who longed for such a curate and others who were encouraged to confess their own inner angst. I share this story last because it further highlights all the steps described above. Because we had spent time together prior to confirming we would like to enter the trainer/trainee relationship, D made it clear that, although she was gifted and experienced, in some aspects of church there were a huge number of things she needed to be taught and declared herself teachable. She also quickly picked up on areas of strength in my own ministry which she discerned as things she needed to develop and hone. The bedrock of this mutual relationship enabled us to minister together with confidence but also, as the years passed, enabled me to deploy her with equal confidence.

The threads that link the four stories

The first common insight in all this is to ask honest, robust questions at the start. The second factor is not to be afraid to take time and not to be pushed into anything by external pressure.

Looking back over four decades and four training experiences, I can reflect that the years when I was a trainer were richer and more enjoyable than when ploughing the furrow without an ordained colleague to unburden to and share myriad insights and planning meetings with. More important even than those things have been the regular gatherings for prayer and the chewing over of the Scriptures of the day. Like all relationships, one enters the training relationship by agreeing to risk the ups and downs and the joys and trials. Sometimes the risk pays off in spades and at others the blessings are more mixed. However, when the wider Church discerned a trainer in me it stirred a thrill of anticipation, and was the beginning of a number of kingdom adventures.

Part 6

THE TRANSITION
FROM CURATE
TO INCUMBENT

21

Rosalyn F. T. Murphy

———•◦•———

Rosalyn is the vicar of St Thomas' Church, Blackpool and serves on the Archbishops' Council. Prior to ordination, she was a postgraduate student at Durham University earning a Master's in Theological Research and a PhD in Biblical Studies. Before theological training she was a Senior Vice-President of Marketing and Fund Development at a leading business charity in Richmond, Virginia (USA). Rosalyn was ordained in Durham and became the first female curate to serve at St Nicholas' Church, Durham, popularly known as 'The Church in the Marketplace', having featured in George Carey's book of that name.

* * *

The transition from curate to incumbent marks a crucial period of discernment and further self-discovery. It indicates the completion of one chapter and the beginning of another. For me, this transition is a 'River Jordan crossing' because while a curate is yet receiving the affirmation and moral support of her training incumbent, she is prayerfully discerning God's direction for her in a very new capacity; all the while continuing her journey onward. I guess, when I put it in English vernacular, my experience could be called a 'River Wear crossing'. I remember making the daily journey over the Milburngate Bridge, walking from the curate's house to St Nicholas' Church in Durham for morning prayers or Sunday services.

Most mornings I took that brief 20-minute walk for granted; the Wear flowed along and my thoughts wandered reflectively on student ministry activities, small-group leaders' training, or the upcoming Christmas fair. Rarely did I consider that one day the return walk would be a final journey where the security of curacy would be left behind as I moved into incumbency.

Now, as I reminisce, being a curate is very much like being Joshua or Caleb. There is a Moses or perhaps even a Miriam mentoring, guiding and directing you along the journey. But eventually, the time comes when you're encouraged to step out on your own, to 'cross over', trusting in God alone to guide and direct you. 'Do not be afraid, stand firm' and see all that God will accomplish for you and through you, in good time (Exodus 14.13).

During the transition period, spiritual direction is essential. However, the ultimate decision in discerning God's direction is yours; for God alone knows his plans for you. As a curate you need to have faith that God has already identified the church, team ministry or chaplaincy that is right for you. And that God has even prepared the people that you'll be called to journey alongside – to affirm, teach, nurture and love. Consequently, the transition from curate to incumbent is a time of intent listening to discover the next step in your ministerial journey.

As a curate in Durham, my experience was cut short somewhat, as during the second year my incumbent accepted a posting to a church in Hong Kong. He had served there before, and now had an opportunity to return as a senior priest. He was ecstatic! However, like Joshua, I wanted to hold on to him and the security his experience and oversight offered. While Hong Kong was not the plains of Moab, Mount Nebo, or even the peaks of Pisgah, it seemed just as far away.

It took a great deal of personal prayer and several meetings with my incumbent before I was able to admit the truth – that I was reluctant to release him to do God's will. In my daily prayers, I seemed to revisit time and again Israel's exodus story and the call of Joshua: 'do not fear or be dismayed . . . go up now . . . I have handed over to you . . . a people . . . a city . . . a land' (Joshua 8.1, NRSV).

At that time, it was difficult for me to acknowledge that I, who had begun my journey as deacon so confident in God's plans for me and assured of his constant presence, now felt abandoned. Perhaps you feel this way too – a bit uncertain if you're hearing God's voice clearly – but don't fret, because God has a way of confirming his plans.

Before my incumbent left for Hong Kong, his prayers and words affirmed and blessed me. On the Friday morning before his final Sunday, we sat in the small chapel praying, a session which was followed by a very lengthy silence. Finally he looked at me and said, 'I wouldn't leave if I didn't have total confidence that you were capable of leading this church without me.' He touched my hand to reassure me and concluded, 'You can do this; you're ready. You will not be alone, God is with you.'

Up until that exact moment, I hadn't felt ready at all. I had drifted into a brief period of self-doubt, questioning my calling and preparedness. Even when hearing God's word to me, at times I believed and other times I doubted. Yet that morning I experienced renewed strength and confidence, as if a huge burden had been lifted off my shoulders. God's calling and the ministry before me was being blessed and affirmed by the one person who represented the 'Moses' in my life – I needed to hear from him that it was time to 'cross over'.

As God would have it, it didn't stop there. Later that day, our church administrator offered to take me out for coffee. We had become very close friends, and I think she too could sense the hesitancy that had stifled my usual confident personality. We were sitting in the Slug and Lettuce chatting away when she too touched my hand and said, 'You're one of the best things that's ever happened to St Nick's. Remember what Archbishop Carey said, you're the type of person he had in mind when he wrote *The Church in the Marketplace*. Listen to the words God has spoken and be confident.'

She was referring to one of the first times I'd preached at our morning service, unaware that the former archbishop had returned to visit his previous parish church. It wasn't until my incumbent introduced me as the preacher that he also welcomed the former archbishop, who as an incumbent had pastored the church. A bit daunted by the announcement, I took a deep breath as I approached the podium, quietly praying my favourite phrase – 'Well, Holy Spirit, here we go.'

To this day, I don't recall the sermon, and what followed remains a blur, but I do remember shaking his hand and thanking him for worshipping with us. For me, his accolades were an affirmation of being exactly where God wanted me. More importantly, I learned something crucial to parish ministry that day. Even as the former archbishop shook my hand, his eye contact and unpretentious engagement was such that I knew he was ministering *directly* to me. For those few minutes I had his utmost attention. While others stood by, he appeared almost unaware of their fidgeting nervousness while awaiting his next move.

Later, upon reflection, the scene seemed reminiscent of the disciples in the gospel narratives, hurrying others along or even discouraging some from approaching Jesus. But Jesus wasn't pressured by the agendas or time schedules others held. He was concerned about God's people; and his 'ministry of presence' dramatically impacted the lives of those he encountered. This was a characteristic I committed to model in future ministry.

Following my incumbent's departure the day-to-day 'busy-ness' increased. I prepared preaching rotas and planned special services, working alongside the numerous non-stipendiary and self-supporting clergy and lay readers. It was an incredible time of learning from some of the most experienced preachers and scholars in the Church of England, as many were employed or retired tutors, lecturers and theological scholars from Durham University. Being part of such a team made me realize the importance of collaboration, and the need for team-building skills in any future incumbency role. A balanced team ensures diverse input during problem-solving or even when designing dynamic liturgy. Both skills – problem-solving and creativity – help to create a healthy atmosphere in which a church can flourish. I recognized the benefit of this 'good mix' more fully when organizing the student ministry's 'Welcome Ceilidh'. I discussed the dance with the student ministry team, as well as the leadership team of ordained and lay readers. The student team suggested that the church's praise band provide the music. They worked on all the practicalities – sending out invitations, distributing flyers, decorations, hospitality. The staff team worked out creative use of every aspect of the building – the lower parish hall was transformed into a wine and cheese bar, the chapel became a coffee and dessert café, while the upper hall became a quiet space with light refreshments, accommodating more intimate conversations.

Alongside this form of creative collaboration, theological and intellectual engagement flourished as we all journeyed together in ministry. I learned that sermons required not only critical exegesis, but also practical application, humour, ingenuity, and from time to time a challenge to move even closer to God.

I encourage every curate to visit other churches whenever possible; to listen to and observe good preachers. Or visit the website of the College of Preachers, identify one or more members in your area, then take time to go, listen and learn from them. Mix it up! If you're an evangelical, visit a cathedral and be attentive to the speaker, to the ambience of the worship and its liturgy. If your tradition is more Anglo-Catholic, visit an evangelical church; examine the expressive preaching styles, sermon content and colourful worship. The breadth of preaching and worship traditions is such that we have much to learn from each other, while God is 'fine-tuning' the style and shape of our own preaching and proclamation.

By the time I entered the transition period from curate to incumbent, I, with my colleagues, parochial church council and church body, had stepped across the 'stone-ridden waters' and rapid whirlpools of an interregnum. There was a parish profile to write, advertisements to place, searches to carry out, applications to review, parish visits to plan and interviews to conduct. When our new vicar arrived I felt fully ready to begin planning God's next step for me, be it priest-in-charge, vicar, associate or team minister.

Any curate who encounters an interregnum can learn so much from the experience. It gave me good insight into the recruitment and selection process, and familiarized me with the various church patrons, such as diocesan bishops, archbishops, cathedrals, the Crown or charitable entities like the Church Pastoral Aid Society (CPAS), Church Patronage Trust and Church Society Trust. When I began searching for my first incumbent's post I looked at two churches – one of them was with CPAS. I was invited to meet with one of the directors there who was also involved in our interregnum and he sent me the full list of church vacancies where CPAS was the patron.

However, he also suggested I contact the person handling Crown appointments because he felt they too might have a vacancy of interest to me. This led to my meeting with an archdeacon in Oxford. So sometimes, simply making contact with one organization can lead to developing contact with another. Also, contact with church patrons will familiarize you with what's on offer outside your diocesan area (especially if you're looking to move elsewhere), and they can put you in contact with archdeacons or bishops who are better aware of current as well as upcoming vacancies. Remember, while this is a time of total dependency on God through prayer and guidance from the Holy Spirit, decision-making is better aided through informal consultations with archdeacons or area deans, and full exploration of what's available that might complement your ministry style, worship tradition and passion.

While prayer and discernment are crucial elements of the transitioning process, so is reflection; something that as curates we sometimes fail to do. Once the new incumbent arrived I realized I had time to review and reflect on my curacy, as well as all of my placements – those experiences that occurred prior to ordination. I had chronicled most of my experiences, expectations and valuable lessons in journals. As I read through many of them, I noticed that my interaction with others had changed. Each individual was important – I was learning to make time to listen and 'be present'.

For instance, prior to ordination I was commissioned to serve alongside a curate in Easington Colliery for ten months. She was serving three small rural churches, and had been there for nearly four years when I arrived. She asked me to assist her as a lay minister, preaching, teaching, deaconing during the Eucharist celebration, and preparing children for Holy Communion and confirmation. The worship tradition of the churches was high Anglo-Catholic, and many elements from my worship experiences in America while attending a Jesuit university (Marquette) were relevant. While the village was economically poor, the Christian communities were rich in faithful, loving service with strength and dedication honed through suffering.

My notes reflected that I had spent very little time listening to the congregation, their needs, fears and community vision. As curates we're often caught up in 'getting the job done', but part of the job is 'being there', listening, hearing, and holding the vision of the congregation in tension with what God is saying until the Holy Spirit successfully blends the two. If you're moving into an incumbency, then be prepared to experience the sacrifice and suffering that builds strength and greater commitment to God's calling, and the time it takes for that to happen. But 'fear not', for God is with you.

Prior to attending the Bishops' Selection Conference, I served in another rural parish in Sunderland Bridge for 18 months. Here too the worship tradition was high Anglo-Catholic. The male incumbent had left the Church of England in opposition to the ordination of women, served several years in the Anglican Church in America, and returned to England to take up the posting. The parish community was affluent and well educated. The colour and vibrancy of the worship, along with the splendid fellowship, was not always extended to the surrounding communities.

While arranging a Lent course, I asked the incumbent if we could open the study group to other churches, as well as to friends and work colleagues. He agreed. The Lent course was well attended by more than ten female members of the congregation, along with friends, family and members from the local Methodist and Baptist churches. Our sitting room was filled to capacity with nearly 30 people – making the study group a tremendous success!

After the Easter break, I met with two women who wanted the group to continue as a bi-weekly Bible study. During the meeting they discussed a desire also to organize an outreach, serving as mentors to young single mothers in the surrounding community. I agreed to assist them in organizing this, and in a few short months some of the young mothers had honed their interpersonal skills and taken on part-time jobs. This poignant experience of Bible study leading to outreach and discipleship reflected the power of the gospel message.

As incumbents we need to confidently expect God's power to move in our communities. Often this means that further training, leadership development and ongoing support for the body of Christ may be needed until this important work takes form and flourishes. Remember, our parishioners are also called by God to help make disciples.

A short placement (six months) prior to ordination was with an evangelical church in Chester-le-Street. It was vibrant and diverse. Modelled on a 'spoke and wheel' concept, small sister cell churches existed in the local working men's club, the school assembly hall and the parish centre. A lively Book of Common Prayer (BCP) congregation, some 200 strong, met each Sunday at 8 a.m. It was followed by a traditional morning prayer service, and a later service of baptism for infants. A New Wine charismatic service was held in the evenings, alongside an evening prayer and healing service.

I served with each congregation before settling in with the BCP worshippers – the contemplative ambience and historical rhythm of the old English liturgy was captivating and spiritually refreshing. And the heartfelt welcome from the congregation was delightful! I recall on the very first Sunday being invited to breakfast by an elderly couple who themselves attended regularly. After a few more invitations this became a Sunday morning ritual where Christian fellowship blended nicely with food; friendship quickly developed.

As an incumbent, the initial welcome to every individual who enters the church informs the attender. First impressions really are lasting – are we insular, set in our ways or part of an inner clique? Or are we open-minded, looking outward, ready to share the good news of the gospel message with those in need of hearing it? As curates, we often take the generous acts of welcome and hospitality for granted, assuming that these things are indigenous to all Christian communities. Many congregations understand the significance of hospitality, welcome, outreach, evangelism and engagement with others for church growth. These gifts and skills are paramount in building the kingdom of God, especially among those in our communities who don't know or experience God's loving kindness in their daily lives. However, sometimes these skills may be lacking and will need to be learnt. As an incumbent one of the most significant characteristics we can model to our congregation(s) is authentic heart renewal – exhibited in our welcoming generosity extended to others.

Today, I can more fully appreciate my curacy journey of training and exploration. While it wasn't exactly 40 years in the Sinai wilderness, it did shape my understanding of the rich liturgical fabric, diverse worship traditions and formal administrative structure that *is* the Church of England. I hoped and prayed that God would lead me to a church where creative liturgies and diverse traditions would merge, where welcoming hospitality would be authentic, and where the congregation would have a heart for mission and outreach. I wanted to 'cross over' the River Jordan (or the River Wear) into a parish land that God had set aside especially for *me*. Today, some six years into my incumbency, I believe that prayer is being answered daily. Sometimes it takes a while, other times it happens more quickly, but 'fear not', you'll get there.

Every aspect of my training – the various lay commissions, theological education, my curacy, and yes, even the interregnum – was part of the transition journey. Through it all, God was shaping and forming my character in preparation for 'crossing over' into something new. My advice: trust that during your curacy God is preparing *you*, and you won't miss out on his ultimate plan for your life.

As an incumbent, I now realize that God gives us opportunities to open doors that have been closed to others: chance encounters with both poor and affluent, and occasions when we can all come together in joyful worship, high or low. God nurtures us through the Holy Spirit, meticulously blending our various liturgical styles, traditions and preaching methods to enhance the individual and corporate worship experience.

This intermingling, when creatively presented and charitably received, gives expression to an opulent tapestry of spiritual worship.

And yet, the best advice I can pass on to any curate is to remember that the 'ministry of presence' prevails. Sometimes silent and listening, other times prayerful and discerning, but always, *always* extending the offer of God's gracious invitation in a way that reveals the importance of the 'other' and draws him or her into the gentle warmth of the love of Christ.

Part 7

DEALING WITH
THORNY ISSUES

22

Howard Worsley

———•◆•———

Howard is the Tutor in Mission at Trinity College in Bristol and a senior lecturer in Christian Education at Canterbury Christchurch University. He is a long-term researcher into children's spirituality, keen to preserve their early perceptions of faith. He has previously worked as a secondary school teacher, a Scripture Union worker, an Anglican vicar (and training incumbent), a university teacher of theology, a diocesan director of education (in Nottingham and then in London) and as a chaplain in both the higher education and further education sectors.

* * *

Introduction

You do not have to travel far in the Church of England to find a story about a difficult curacy, though many of these stories are hidden from the public domain. Many curates find the early period of ministry to be a challenging time, and similarly it is a poorly concealed secret that a lot of training incumbents do not sufficiently value their curates. This chapter will not attempt to offer any blame for the number of curacy breakdowns that have occurred (and which are happening even now), nor of the many unresolved issues that still exist, but it will reflect on why such breakdowns happen. It will then proceed to reflect on how to deal with those 'thorny issues'.

For the curate, it can be frustrating to be the junior member of the team, especially when in a previous life he or she might have occupied a more senior professional role. The curate may also have skills and experiences beyond those of his or her vicar colleague. It is also likely that for those curates who are on a stipend after training in a residential context, their arrival in the 'real world' of the parish brings considerable expectations and a desire for an idealized life involving prayer, a hope for fulfilling and strategic Christian relationships and a sense of God's kingdom being seen on earth. Those curates who are non-stipendiary and who have maintained a job while they were being trained will come expecting collegiality and partnership in ministry.

The reality might be very different. Instead of being valued and usefully employed, the curate may find herself overlooked, not adequately communicated with and generally deskilled (see Swift, 'How Should Health Care Chaplaincy Negotiate its Professional Identity?' and Berry, 'The Social Construction of the Ministry Student').

For the incumbent, it might be irritating to have a new colleague who seems to know many things he or she does not deem relevant, to have ideas about time off or new ways of working and to be ambitious for a spiritual life. It is quite possible for the arrival of a new curate to threaten the incumbent's previous way of working and take up a lot of that precious commodity called time. It is also not unheard of for a gifted curate to unwittingly make an established incumbent feel insecure. To have a curate is likely to have been a long-held desire for partnership in the gospel, but the incumbent may not have thought through the issues of training and the need for a new pattern of communicating. Instead of finding a close colleague, the incumbent gains a new and unlooked-for responsibility and reverts to previous negative experiences of being a curate, or to his or her own deeper insecurity.

Of course, the experience for both curate and incumbent might be entirely opposite to what I am suggesting, but that is a different chapter, which might have been called 'The ideal of good partnerships in ministry'. Since I will be focusing on how to deal with thorny issues, it might better be called 'How to cope when things go wrong'.

Previous research in thorny issues from curacy experience

My own Director of Post-Ordination Training, Dr Neil Burgess, published in 1998 a book entitled *Into Deep Water*. It was an in-depth study of 20 people ordained as deacons between 1989 and 1994, and included anonymous stories and experiences told verbatim by curates. Burgess exposed the issue of mismatched expectations (on both sides), sometimes caused or exacerbated by less-than-clear job descriptions, as a major faultline. Overall the book showed the paradox whereby huge motivation on the part of curates was tempered by an institutional suppression that affected lifestyles, family relationships and inner peace.

Although Burgess's book is more than 15 years old, the experiences of curates across the country since then have supported his main narrative. I have personally been involved in supporting many curates who were trying to survive when the structures felt inadequate. Many ordinands whom I taught at theological college have kept in touch as their careers have developed, and as a result I have heard the joys and sorrows of different curates – and the responses made by different dioceses to the difficulties.

Current case studies in thorny issues

In order to prepare for this chapter, I invited several people who are currently curates to share their stories confidentially with me, and I have received back stories of people who continue to testify to the 'thorny issues' that arise. From these I have selected two case studies written by curates in 2013.

Rachel's story

The first titled her story 'An account of curacy breakdown'. It is told from the perspective of the curate, Rachel, and her vicar colleague is James.

> A couple of weeks later, having observed nothing of James' ministry, and not knowing where he spent most of his days, he handed me a funeral referral, and told me, 'There you go, it's an easy one. Just go and see the family and use the book, you'll be fine.' His definition of training carried on in this vein. There was virtually no observation, and he resented being asked to go over things, telling me he couldn't understand why intelligent people needed support. Fortunately for me, I had enough friends in ministry to draw on their experience and support. But I almost never saw James one to one, we did not look at the curate training framework, he refused to draw up an annual working agreement, and generally curtailed supervision, cancelled it, or refused to schedule it altogether.
>
> He dumped a wedding couple on me for me to see, without guidance on what to do. When I observed a wedding interview he did, he said he wanted me to do the wedding. I pointed out the date was that of my priesting – he said he expected me to come and do the wedding in the afternoon then go back to my priesting in the evening, and was surprised and angry when I pointed out I would be on ordination retreat. The first baptism I did, he did not introduce me to the family beforehand, and did not introduce me during the service. He did not even give me the names of the children I was going to baptize, even though I had asked repeatedly.

This particular story cannot be dismissed as being simply the mismatch of naive expectations of a young curate or the lack of life experience of someone new to the Church, nor can it be treated as merely being one-sided. It reveals serious problems of a bullying nature which are likely to be deep-seated on the part of the incumbent. It also details issues of ecclesiastical illegalities concerning presiding at the Eucharist and the registration of a wedding.

As the story continues, it evidences how the internal machinery of the diocese was unable to take effective action due to the difference between the diocesan bishop's pastoral style and the archdeacon's more robust style of action. It also raises functional issues of how the bishop decides where and who will be the training parish and training incumbent, and whether the training incumbent actually receives training for the task:

> Time rolled on and no paperwork, no evaluations were done, and the inevitable arrived – the director of curate training again checked on what was going on. The Archdeacon became involved. When James discovered I had talked to the Archdeacon, he became more angry and bullying. I was concerned that he was going to lie, and I spoke to my Archdeacon to flag this, and gave him a detailed list of (non)supervisions, with dates, and of incidents of concern. James predictably lied, but got caught up in his own lies so that they were obvious to the Archdeacon . . .
>
> He made me meet with him, and was bullying, and lied to my face – repeatedly. This was the point at which I knew I had to leave. He then took it upon himself to attack me on everything he could. He could not fault my 'performance' so he attacked me on the fact I was doing further doctoral study. I pointed out I had done no work on it – he then berated me for doing a Hebrew class on my day off, and neglecting my family!
>
> I was due to see the Archdeacon on that day, and I laid everything on the table. The Archdeacon was extremely supportive, and told me that what I was saying was almost word for word the kind of account they had heard during the pastoral breakdown previously. He also said he was aware James lied routinely, this had been picked up independently. He apologized for placing me there in the first place, and told me he was pulling me out with immediate effect . . .

Looking back, Rachel then comments:

> While the Archdeacon would have dealt with the matter much more robustly, the bishop went with a more 'pastoral' approach – despite the continued harassment I have had to suffer.

This account flags issues that are even more complex and details that the duplicity was previously known to the diocesan authorities, and that this institutional awareness had not resulted in prior action. Faced with this the curate could easily feel disillusioned and be tempted to accept the role of victim.

I am pleased that in this instance, a change in curacy resulted in the deacon being happily placed elsewhere, but left her with a more worldly-wise attitude to the Church. This could be because with the recently applied 'assessment at the end of curacy' the training of curates is now much more procedurally tracked. Rachel's story concludes:

> As I look back, I think the diocese has been very supportive of me. I received a lot of kindness and support from my Archdeacon and both Bishops. They also apologized unreservedly for placing me with James when there were concerns already, but they said, 'We thought that if anyone could handle him, you could!' Clearly, they were wrong. I was hugely disappointed however that very little happened in way of disciplinary sanctions towards James despite the amount of hard evidence, and the fact that this was the fourth documented case of bullying. I appreciate I did not know exactly what had been done or not, but it seems to me that I bore the brunt of things, had to move, and was asked not to tell my story to anyone, and so had to cope with the rumours and nastiness that James has spread since. The congregation was not fooled – I received a lot of encouragement, and many letters of support on my behalf were written to the bishop. The whole incident has shaken my trust in the Church and, I have to say, in the integrity of its senior leaders.

This last section offers the suggestion that the diocese was previously aware of the incumbent's inadequacies as a bully and was unable to act decisively (though quite what it had done was unknown to the curate). More tellingly, the implicit culture of heroic individualism is mentioned by way of flattery: 'We thought that if anyone could handle him, you could!' This comment also reveals the current shifting culture within the Church of England, which, while becoming increasingly more professionalized and objectively accountable, remains one in which senior clergy might still offer comments that could lead to litigation if proved to be accurate. Rachel is left intact but feeling somewhat disillusioned due to the way the diocese closed rank on how it handled the wider issues, leaving her ignorant of the wider institutional response.

Peter's story

The second case study details the experiences of Peter, who had the misfortune of two sequential failed curacies and tells a story that is extremely disconcerting.

His first curacy was a pioneer minister post – an associate vicar's role that had been unsuccessfully advertised twice, but which the archdeacon was prepared to change to a training curacy role for the right candidate.

It involved a parish with the exciting prospect of having a large new housing estate being built on its boundary and which had brokered an agreement that the new Church of England primary school constructed on the estate would also host a Sunday church plant. However, things were not as they appeared. He records:

> The first Sunday after my ordination I was pulled aside by lay members and by the associate vicar of the parish and they began to explain and apologize for what they saw as a deliberate deception that had taken place [at the interview for the curacy].

It transpired that there was no church plant, nor had a team been formed to undertake or lead one, though a website for the church plant had been created and was up and running. The person who had been introduced in the interview process as a leader of the church plant had not been involved in the new pioneer appointment, and was quite upset at the deception he had felt pressured into maintaining. Peter discovered that the diocese had released funds for the initial purchase of furniture for the church plant and that it understood the parish to be committed to identifying further finance for other necessities in return for a 'free' centrally funded pioneer minister post.

Despite this mismatch between the reality and what he had been led to believe, Peter went ahead and formed a small group on the estate, which began meeting as the beginnings of a core team for a church plant. It saw its tasks as being to work on prayer and planning for what the church might look like. People in the group wanted to give money on a regular basis for the beginnings of church activities on the estate, but there was no mechanism to do so apart from giving to the main parish church. Peter was then instructed not to restrict donations from the church plant to the estate, but that all giving was 'unrestricted general giving' to the parish. He records:

> My family and I had moved house to this area and knew few people outside the parish situation. Local deanery clergy seemed friendly but there were huge political divisions and I had been instructed by my incumbent not to speak about the situation with them. The Archdeacon was on long-term sick leave. By this point, I too was struggling with stress and had rolled from one infection and virus to another. I was utterly exhausted and run-down. The Bishop asked if I would be willing to ask my GP to sign me off for a couple of weeks to give him time to consider how best to address the situation. I agreed and took a fortnight off. At the end of this period, the Bishop said that he didn't think that the

post should really exist given that there wasn't a church plant in existence, and that he didn't think it should be a training curacy. He explained that it would not be straightforward to transfer my post as it hadn't been created from a normal curacy post, but said that there were a couple of possibilities for a move within the area. He also explained that to be able to move me, I would need to technically resign from the existing role. At his request, I then did this.

Peter's resignation only made matters worse, because after he had received it, the bishop became 'suddenly distant' and the stipend dried up. Peter's situation was only addressed when he moved to another area and was offered a different curacy, this time in a non-stipendiary capacity.

Reflecting on this it is clear that the incoming curate to a new form of ministry must check in detail what is expected and how the lines of accountability are to work. It appears that when a visionary post is considered, it may be rather 'more imagined than actual', and if this is so, it is the pioneer curate who has to cope with that discrepancy. The communication between a diocesan structure and a local parish is rarely as transparent as it appears on the outside, as the structures are so flexible as to be very disconcerting when immediate intervention is required.

It is interesting to note that policy requires pioneer curates to be supervised by the training incumbent (accountable to the training depart-ment) *and* another person with pioneer qualifications (accountable to the mission or like department), a requirement that should therefore 'protect' the curate. Moreover curacy is a training post, and (in theory) any actual projects, like church planting, should not be the focus of the curacy. The curacy is there to train the participant in the tasks to which he or she will be deployed *after* curacy.

Peter's first curacy was reviewed and he was moved back into a new post under the direct authority of a diocesan bishop, and so was effectively delegated to archdeacons. He had learnt from his previous experience and approved a working agreement at the outset with his new training incumbent that stated that he was able to work full-time during school terms and part-time in school holidays, but that this arrangement could be revised at a later date if family commit-ments or financial needs changed. However, he was again to experience difficulties:

My training incumbent, Vicky, became disparaging about my insistence on holding boundaries for family time in accordance with my working agreement, but I stood my ground because of

my wife's work. Then a financial storm broke. It transpired that
the parish was massively in deficit and the worship leader was
made redundant. The children's worker walked out. The pastoral
assistant was told that her contract would not be renewed, and
the administrator's days were cut. I was given responsibility for
children's church 'because I was a dad' and expected to provide
craft resources, etc. out of my own pocket. Everything I did – from
Alpha courses to pastoral phone calls – I had to pay for myself.
I ran from service to service, running children's work, preaching
and leading. I was still waiting to be priested, which Vicky said
she would sort out . . . but never did. I became used to her last-
minute absences, late-night emails and destructive behaviour.
We had not had a supervision meeting in several months when
my family learned that my wife's income was going to be less
that year than had been expected. I needed to earn some
money or we would need to move house again. When I asked
Vicky for my working hours to be reduced (as I was entitled
to do, given my SSM status) she was harsh and threatening –
talking about how part-time she regarded me as already being.

This story details how the financial situation, as well as the clarity of work
expectations, affects a curacy. In this instance, the curacy director also
failed the curate in not imposing national and diocesan policy regarding
standard expectations for curacy agreements, which are not the responsibility of the training incumbent but agreed by the sponsoring bishop
and 'enforced' by the curacy director.

Essentially, this new curacy too was to break down irretrievably despite
the presence of a mentor and despite early attempts at reconciliation.
What particularly hurt Peter was for him to open the *Church Times* one
day and to see his name announced in the 'Resignations' column, even
though he had not resigned.

At the time of writing, Peter felt deeply aggrieved, sensing that the
diocesan system was set up to preserve the status quo and did not address
any of the deeper structural or sexist issues that he deemed to be present.
His own future in ministry was under threat, with no guarantee that he
would ever return to ministry. He reflected that:

The definition of 'fair' within the Church takes no account of
basic power narratives. As a criminologist with specialisms in
reconciliation and restorative justice, I found it striking how a
curate and training incumbent were repeatedly treated as if
both were in equal positions of power – whereas a curate is
entirely vulnerable and reliant on a system which can leave
them homeless and without income at a stroke. I found that

the Desmond Tutu quote kept coming to mind throughout both processes: 'If you are neutral in situations of injustice, you have chosen the side of the oppressor. If an elephant has its foot on the tail of a mouse and you say that you are neutral, the mouse will not appreciate your neutrality.'

He also reflected that:

The Church has a terror of legal action against it, yet repeatedly breaches its own procedures. In the case of my second curacy, I at no point put anything in writing that constituted resignation, and neither has any written record of any meeting been circulated or agreed. Yet my 'resignation' was published. I am still considering my response to this, and would like to do whatever is necessary to see that no curate is treated so poorly and unlawfully again.

Dealing with thorny issues

Having articulated some of the issues and how they arise, it is important now to consider how *a curate* might cope with them at a personal level and also to offer reflection as to how *the institution* can offer better structural process at a corporate level.

Personal survival

At a deep level we are personally responsible for our lives and we stand alone before God. Therefore we need to recognize and 'own' whatever happens to us, so that we are not brought down by adverse circumstances. This is what prevents us both from becoming entirely powerless and being victimized by life events or by cultural oppression, and from losing the last protection against being bullied. It is not an excuse for any unjust external factors that might bear upon us, but it is a reminder that we cannot deal with all the historical circumstances that have brought about the present predicament, and indeed we do not fully understand all the issues causing it. It is the spiritual balance that allows us to pray the Serenity Prayer:

God grant me the serenity
to accept the things I cannot change;
courage to change the things I can;
and wisdom to know the difference.

Commenting on this prayer, the theologian Reinhold Niebuhr reputedly wrote a subsequent prayer:

Living one day at a time;
Enjoying one moment at a time;
Accepting hardships as the pathway to peace;
Taking, as He did, this sinful world
as it is, not as I would have it;
Trusting that He will make all things right
if I surrender to His Will;
That I may be reasonably happy in this life
and supremely happy with Him
Forever in the next.
Amen.

I have often pondered on the similarities between having a fatalistic theology and having a theology of submission to a loving God, and the distinction is to do with how we relate to God as opposed to how we act. Should we simply accept things that go wrong or do we fight everything? How this is answered is often dependent on theological tradition. If a curate is caught out in the complexity of life, drawn by her own sense of calling and a belief in a God who loves her, but finds herself trapped within a context that is beyond her, it is vital for her to develop resilience (see Allain-Chapman, *Resilient Pastors*) and to remain spiritually centred.

Be spiritually centred

At a core level the curate is answerable to God, and this must always be recognized if a spiritual balance is to be maintained. The example of St Francis of Assisi is helpful, in that he was remarkable for showing humility when facing huge odds. Francis lived in an age when the Church was significantly corrupted by wealth and immorality, but he trusted that God had given him the task of mission and he set about rebuilding the Church. He always deferred both to the episcopate and to the clergy, never feeling worthy to be ordained himself. Even when clerics were other than perfect, he found the grace to respect them and to work with them by reminding himself of Christ's love for him. He would pray the prayer that we now know by his name:

May the power of your love,
Fiery and sweet as honey,
Wean our hearts
From all that is evil.
Grant us to die for the love of your love,
You who were so good as to die
For the love of our love,
Amen.

Be adaptable

In the marketplace of business, the companies that survive are those that learn to adapt to the flux in the market. This is often known as 'being agile'. Companies that have not changed sufficiently cease to trade or need to downscale, and on the high street it is clear that this has happened to Woolworth, Marks and Spencer and the Post Office. In the ecclesial world of Church, we are not just a business, but we do need to learn how to adapt to the changes in religious attitude, to market forces and to postmodern styles of belonging. The curate (as well as the incumbent and the diocesan structure) needs to learn how to respond to these various external influences.

The curate is called upon to be an agent of change and to stand at the crossroads of an older and traditional world (the Church) and the newer and passing world of transience (culture). He must be theologically reflective but must not take sole responsibility for effecting that change, though he will be part of it. His prayer must be like that attributed to another Francis, Sir (not Saint) Francis Drake, whom history presents as an adaptable navigator and cultural entrepreneur of the sixteenth century:

> Disturb us, Lord, when
> We are too pleased with ourselves,
> When our dreams have come true
> Because we dreamed too little,
> When we arrived safely
> Because we sailed too close to the shore.
>
> Disturb us, Lord, when
> With the abundance of things we possess
> We have lost our thirst
> For the waters of life;
> Having fallen in love with life,
> We have ceased to dream of eternity
> And in our efforts to build a new earth,
> We have allowed our vision
> Of the new Heaven to dim.
>
> Disturb us, Lord, to dare more boldly,
> To venture on wilder seas
> Where storms will show Your mastery;
> Where losing sight of land,
> We shall find the stars.
>
> We ask you to push back
> The horizons of our hopes;

And to push back the future
In strength, courage, hope, and love.

This we ask in the name of our Captain,
Who is Jesus Christ.

Reject the falsehood of platitude

The deep-seated nature of the thorny issues affecting curates suggests that a quick fix is unlikely and that organizational change is necessary. Changing an organization means having a vision for changing the culture, and this in turn means re-evaluating that culture.

As these values are identified, we must fight off the half-truths and the platitudes currently evident in the Church. Back in 1998, in Burgess's final chapter, 'What is Happening and What can be Done?', he identified three falsehoods (pp. 133–7):

1 What have curates got to worry about? (*The presumption being that Church life is rarefied and without trauma.*)
2 It's only for a few years! (*The notion that curates can endure their lot because it will pass.*)
3 This can only be resolved by a new training programme! (*The half-truth that suggests a single piece of training will remedy the problem.*)

It is worth reflecting on what current half-truths and platitudes exist in the second decade of the twenty-first century. They might be as follows:

- The Church has too much personal trauma dealing with issues in human sexuality or gender issues in episcopacy to be bothered about curacy problems. (*The presumption that the Church is too beleaguered to handle any other sensitive matters. This also betrays the lie that curates are not valuable.*)
- IME (Initial Ministerial Education) I–VII has got this covered. (*The belief that recent attempts to re-evaluate initial ministerial education have dealt with everything affecting curacy.*)
- New moves to bring about the CDM (clergy discipline measure) can handle all matters of conflict. (*The notion that other recent change occurring is fully embedded within the Church.*)

If the falsehood of platitude is to be rejected, a new realism must be accepted. In the case of the curacy experience in the Church of England, realism means noting that the historic Church is essentially patriarchal, hierarchal and slow to change. These factors can easily combine to bring about a structure that is abusive to its most vulnerable clergy, especially those lowest in the hierarchal system.

Organizational change

Theologically it is necessary to believe that we are part of Christ's body, even though the structural organization of the corporate ecclesial body can sometimes be abusive. Therefore the curate needs not only to survive but to have the belief that the Church can change and learn from its inadequacies.

At the point of writing, there is evidence that the Church of England is putting energy and resource into working for better practice, as seen for example in reviews of common tenure and the common curriculum. Another encouraging move is towards the accountability of clergy, which is probably the most crucial change leading towards the assessment at the end of curacy.

Other areas for organizational change that will help to eradicate thorny issues for curates are:

Clarity of expectations

In the last decade, the training process has become clearer, detailing the competences required for ministerial practice. However, considerable variables exist in the first appointments process, from the point of initial advertising to the curacy agreement between the incumbent and the curate. Future clarity should attempt to detail how the structure works, including the various roles of the bishop, the archdeacon, the diocesan training officer, the incumbent and the curate.

Training and selection of 'training incumbents'

The role of curate is largely a trainee role that may entail being given further responsibilities, but this is not universally known by training incumbents, some of whom offer no training or supervision or even partnered reflection or collegiality. Each diocese needs to have a system of identifying 'training incumbents' and then of monitoring and evaluating them.

Having a proper grievance procedure

However mature and experienced the partnership of curate and incumbent, there will always be difficult issues to handle and therefore an identifiable procedure should be made explicit early on. This will not only involve the relationship between curate and incumbent but also include the possible involvement of parish and diocese. It is helpful to be aware of the possibility of mediation training or of conflict resolution. A key resource here is the Mennonite Bridge Building training course.

Seen from the current context of 'dealing with thorny issues', it appears that the experience of twenty-first-century curacy practice in the Church of England is nothing new. What is clear is that we are called upon to 'carry treasure in earthen vessels' (2 Corinthians 4.7, KJV) and that we do so as a body representing Christ's broken body. We need to do so in partnership with each other and as followers of the Risen Christ who teaches forgiveness and new starts and who breathes hope for the future. We also need to be committed to realism, to the creation of better processes and to the coming of the kingdom of God.

Part 8

THE VALUE OF SHARING STORIES AND SOME PRACTICAL ADVICE

23

The value of sharing stories

JONATHON ROSS-McNAIRN

———•◆•———

'What really is the point in sharing our stories?' asked one of the contributors to this book. It is a good question! After all, the book *is* a collection of personal stories and reflections relating to the experience of being a curate. This chapter is a brief response to that question and makes essentially two points. The first is that the Church should say 'yes' to a culture of learning *through* story. The second is that it is vital that the Church says 'yes' to a more balanced proclamation of the gospel – *by word* and deed.

The Church saying 'yes' to a culture of learning through story

We believe that there is a real value in sharing stories because we can learn from each other's experiences and reflections. If someone were to ask you, 'What is it really like being a Church of England curate?' we hope that you will feel a little more informed as a result of this book. I wonder what sort of words you might use in response? Would you say that it is a privilege, fun, challenging, puzzling, disappointing, rewarding, joyful, or just plain odd?

The precise nature of *what* we learn will, of course, differ for each of us, depending on our context and the questions and assumptions we bring to the text of the story. If you are an ordinand or curate the stories in this book may help you to feel more prepared for the reality of ordained life. They may also encourage you to think through some unexpected areas, such as how people will behave towards you when you are 'the vicar'. I have a friend who, before ordination, would tell me rude (and sometimes funny) jokes but now can't quite bring himself to tell me those sorts of jokes any more (despite my encouragement!). Similarly, if you are a training incumbent, some of the insights of Jonathan Perkin, Alan Howe and Paul Butler will – we hope – encourage you to ask the question, 'What can I learn from their reflections of the incumbent/curate relationship?'

The point is that no one story will be read, interpreted and reflected upon in quite the same way by two different people. This is the value of learning *through* the use of story. It is personal, non-prescriptive and related to situational factors. Indeed, the possibilities for what we might learn seem endless. Would, for example, our reflections from a particular story be the same if we were to read it again in a few years' time? The answer is almost definitely 'no', because our context changes and therefore the questions we have will be different. When I was newly ordained I was particularly occupied with questions such as, 'Where do I stand in church?' 'What do I wear?' 'Does my sermon make any sense at all?' and 'When will they find me out?' Now, as I approach the end of my curacy, I have a different set of questions (although those earlier questions do reappear now and again).

The question of what we learn from people's stories is, of course, much more than simply being informed or acquiring knowledge (as important as this is). We also hope that they will be a source of inspiration and challenge. Might they broaden your horizons a little, challenge misconceptions and encourage all of us to take risks in the service of Christ and his Church. For example, Rob Kean's chapter reflecting on his ministry in the pub may enable us to think more carefully about the ordained person's charge to share in the 'cure of souls' for the whole parish (and indeed whether a round of drinks is a legitimate ministerial expense!).

As we read about the experiences of others in ministry, we might be able to reflect on the nature of our own ministry and this may (or perhaps 'should') confront us with some challenging and disturbing questions. If you are a curate or vicar you might ask yourself, in what ways are you making the gospel *actually good news* in your community? Are we really listening to the stories of people in our parishes? During my curacy, I remember finding myself at a funeral wake in a Jamaican club, eating saltfish (delicious) and drinking rum (they insisted – delicious too), listening to the stories of that community. I didn't understand some of the finer cultural points (for which I apologized at the time), but I was there and I was listening.

The value of sharing stories may also be felt by your being encouraged and affirmed. How important this is! I remember, pre-ordination, being let loose to do an Alpha talk at my church in north London. I don't think I prepared that well and my delivery felt a little dry and uninspiring. The first words the curate said to me after my talk? 'Well done! That was brilliant!' And he pointed out with great enthusiasm all that was good about the talk. He waited until the next day in order to tactfully and sensitively suggest ways in which I might improve. We all need to be encouraged, and the clergy are no exception. Rachel Wilson's chapter too calls us to focus on what we can do rather than what we are unable to do. I am very aware of what I am not very good at (DIY, maths and resisting chocolate come to mind), but thankfully God calls us as we are with our particular gifts and limitations, and as Liz Palin concludes, 'God who calls you *is* faithful.' We feel that it is important (training incumbents, please take note!) that all men and women called to the ordained life may hear the voice of affirmation and assurance and – vitally – the voice that says God *is* there despite the challenges.

The shared experiences in this book may also – we pray – foster a sense of exploration, discovery and hopeful expectation in mission and ministry. Might we be more pioneering and see the landscape in which we live and work as a 'Holy Playground', as Steve Clarke puts it. How can we 'reimagine' mission and ministry in our communities? God calls us to proclaim the gospel afresh and with confidence and joy. As Jonathan Perkin rightly points out, there are far too many gloomy clergy about the place (if I have been one of them, I unreservedly apologize). We hope that you will feel energized and inspired by the stories of others who have been prepared to take risks for the sake of the gospel.

We can also see the value of sharing stories in that they underline the importance of relationships. Through the sharing of our life experiences with others, a real sense of connection and togetherness can happen and meaningful relationships of trust, vulnerability and confidence can be formed. This in turn promotes unity among people and – it follows – comm*unity*. Bruce Goodwin's chapter speaks powerfully about a whole community being brought together as they lived through the story of the death of the Revd John Suddards. This was in large measure enabled by people coming together through the sharing and exploring of their experiences and questions.

When we listen carefully to each other's stories we may also learn something about the presence of God in our lives. Ruth Fitter reflects on the conversation she had with a woman in her church. She writes that in the telling of 'my own story she could see that God was in her story'. It is a moment of revelation – God is there in her life. God is at work through the sharing of stories.

All those engaged in Christian ministry, whether ordained or not, have – we would suggest – a special charge to listen to the experiences of people in their care. Indeed, we would urge the whole people of God to promote a culture within the Church of learning and reflection through the use of storytelling, and we would encourage all clergy to take a lead in modelling this and enabling others to do the same. We just might be surprised by what we learn!

The Church saying 'yes' to a more balanced proclamation of the gospel – by word and deed

We believe that the value of sharing stories goes further still in that it is vital to the mission of the Church. So we turn now – briefly – to some theology.

Newbigin in *The Gospel in a Pluralist Society* suggests (p. 15) that 'The way we understand human life depends on what conception we have of the human story. What is the real story of which my life story is part?' The Christian faith offers us this 'real story' – the story told in the Bible. N. T. Wright in *The New Testament and the People of God* concludes (pp. 41–2) that 'The whole point of Christianity is that it offers a story which is the story of the whole world. It is public truth.'

Central to the Christian faith is the story of God's plan for the world focused in the life, death and resurrection of Jesus Christ. It is a story which has partly been revealed through the biblical witness and – vitally – *is being revealed* through God's ongoing activity in the world today. This 'ongoing activity' is to redeem the whole of creation and is the mission of God.

The Church's task is and always has been to discern the ongoing activity of God in the world and then to participate. Mission by the Church, then, is an 'entering into the life of God', a response to what God is already doing. In *The Mission and Ministry of the Whole Church*, the 2007 report by the Church of England Faith and Order Advisory Group, we read:

> The Church does not introduce Jesus Christ into a situation where he was previously absent, for he is ahead of every action of the Church and does not need the Church's permission to be present. Christ is present, is at work, and is found by many in every place and time, through the universal salvific activity of the Holy Spirit.

Consequently, the question is, 'How can we work out what God is already doing so that the Church can join in?' We argue that it is *through listening to each other's stories and experiences that the presence and movement of God in the world may be discerned.*

The Church today finds itself in a context in which mission and evangelism are an imperative, and in recent times there has naturally been a great deal of thinking in this area. One of the key questions has been, 'How can the gospel be proclaimed in such a way that it connects with today's society?' There are, of course, no easy or straightforward answers but in recent theological thought there has been, in our view, a marked emphasis on the gospel being proclaimed principally by what we do – *our actions.*

Tomlin, for example, persuasively argues the case in *The Provocative Church*. He writes (p. 168) that as members of the Church our task is 'to learn to live the Christian life before we talk about it; to walk the walk, before we talk the talk'. The argument is that a credible Christian community living in unity and modelling the Christian life will *provoke* people to ask about the beliefs that inspire that community. As Newbigin says in *The Gospel in a Pluralist Society*, it is the local Christian congregation that is the 'hermeneutic of the gospel . . . a congregation of men and women who believe it and live by it' (p. 227).

We certainly must believe and live by the gospel, but integral to this is the Church giving a clear and unapologetic voice to the unfolding story of God. The spoken word *is* powerful. The story of God *is* powerful. Our stories *are* powerful. Listening to the stories of people in our communities *is* powerful. Why? Because *God is in the story* waiting to be discovered. We therefore want to urge all people of God to a more balanced proclamation of the gospel – *by word* and deed. We are not called to be a silent provocative Church. Let the story of God be heard with confidence and joy! The Church has a great story to tell – the one true story of God already active in the world, active in our communities, active in our lives. And that is why we must, *must* share our stories.

24

Some practical advice

SONIA BARRON

———•◦•◆•◦•———

Sonia was born in Jamaica but has lived in England since the age of eight. She has worked as a teacher in secondary schools and higher education institutions, and extensively within the broader Church. She was formerly adviser to the Archbishops' Council and is now a curate and vocations adviser in the Diocese of Southwell and Nottingham.

* * *

Map, tent, compass, Bible, machete, powder compact . . . on any journey you make, you will consider beforehand what you need to take with you. And, as we hope this book has illustrated, a curacy is both a journey in itself and part of a greater journey. You'll have noticed that many of the diverse stories included here reveal a move towards greater self-discovery, self-awareness or spiritual growth, and we trust that sharing in the experiences of others who have travelled the road you are now on may prove illuminating and reassuring.

> Deacons are ordained so that the people of God may be better equipped to make Christ known. Theirs is a life of visible self-giving. Christ is the pattern of their calling and their commission; as he washed the feet of his disciples, so they must wash the feet of others.

These words from the beginning of the Ordinal imply that a curacy won't be straightforward. The Christian life isn't like that. 'Self-giving' and washing feet require a degree of sacrifice, and curates certainly need to be aware of, and prepared for, the cost involved to themselves and to their families.

Before you start

What we have called your 'greater journey' began when you first responded to the call to ordained ministry. It will form you as you travel

146

and will continue beyond retirement. So before you begin your curacy you should check, so far as possible, what you are letting yourself in for and whether it will give you the best preparation for your calling.

Talk things through with your potential training incumbent. Remember Alan Howe's advice (given from the perspective of the incumbent, but in many ways applicable to curates too) to listen to your inner voice when it does not feel right, while there is still time to withdraw. Some of the 'loyalty questions' are relevant too; do you think the incumbent will be honest if things start to go wrong, will she affirm you appropriately, and even do you trust her? Alan advises us to be clear from the start about the nature of the potential relationship: 'if [it] is more of an arranged marriage than an ideal partnership of complementary minds, admit it and double check that you can both live with that.'

Ruth Fitter warns of the importance of having the self-awareness, and the courage, to say if the 'fit' doesn't feel right. Her experience highlights how vital it is that you spend time alone with God, so that the other voices – of college tutors, spouses, family, friends, work colleagues, other clergy and potential parishioners – can be silenced for a while, and the still small voice of calm be heard above the clamour of our busy lives.

Establish proper personal spiritual disciplines, says Howard Worsley as he considers some of the thorny issues that may arise during a curacy and gives some sound advice on personal survival. We are personally responsible for our lives, and we stand alone before God; so whatever happens to us we need to recognize and 'own'.

Make sure you have your boundaries in place (not inviolable ones though!). Writing from the perspective of a DDO, Sue Hemsley-Halls says that as well as talking things through in advance, curate and training incumbent should have an understanding of how things can be sorted out if their circumstances or needs change. The working agreement between them should include something about later negotiations if one of the parties isn't happy. It is important that curates are aware of the proper processes if they encounter problems.

There is much to look forward to. Speaking as a training incumbent, Jonathan Perkin writes: 'Curates come to us as prophets. They have vision, enthusiasm, perspective, energy and talent. The Church of England desperately needs them to retain that prophetic edge if it is to survive.' Talk about your gifts and what you can offer to this crucial relationship and what you hope to learn from your training incumbent.

During the journey

Of course it is important that boxes are ticked to show that the person has been exposed to different experiences of ministry and is competent in a wide range of ministries (and more than competent in some of them!). But 'God save us from the "target" culture which produces the right outcomes but with the wrong people,' writes Jonathan Perkin again.

Remain loyal in public. Ruth Worsley stresses the importance of the loyalty that takes over in public following the full and frank discussion in private: 'Once a decision was reached, however, it was clear that we would each support the other in the direction decided upon. We presented a united front in PCC meetings or when required to give a lead. This didn't mean that there was no room for debate or discussion, to which we each contributed, but it did mean that we didn't leave room for the undermining of the other.'

Thrash out problems with the training incumbent in private. For curates who come to ministry from the secular world more experienced and qualified, it can be easy to belittle your training incumbent in public, particularly if you find yourself in a situation where you are feeling frustrated by his or her lack of leadership or action. Both training incumbents in their chapters have pointed to respect as a vital quality in the curate/trainer relationship. Jonathan Perkin explains that respect includes acceptance, tolerance, admiration, forgiveness, affirmation, believing in and valuing the other; but that it also means loving the other person enough to confront, challenge, question, direct and suggest – don't be afraid to do that in an appropriate way.

We are first and foremost disciples of Christ, says Paul Butler, and as a bishop he wants to see ministers of the gospel growing into Christlikeness in their life and ministry. Inevitably, as Christian pilgrims we will have many ups and downs, highs and lows, joys and sorrows, but because we know Immanuel, we can be sure that we are not alone as we set off.

Don't be afraid to say that it's not working. It's a hard thing to do because it seems as if you are admitting that you have failed. Be honest and have the conversation. Jacqueline Stober believes: 'You really only need three things to help you through difficult times: some very good friends who will love you and affirm your gifts; a foundation of robust spiritual practices such as prayer, meditation, reflection; plus a little faith that the God who called you will sustain you no matter what life may bring.'

Sue Hemsley-Halls recognizes that if difficulties can't be resolved even though process is followed properly, the pain can be minimized. Both curate and trainer need to be supported; when things go wrong any sense of failure is usually felt by all. There should be no private or public apportioning of blame.

Don't lose engagement with the wider Church. Attending your deanery chapter provides a forum for you to hear how others are doing and responding to issues that arise at diocesan level. Get involved where you can – find your particular area of interest and look for opportunities to serve on a committee, join a working group on a specific project, stand for election for diocesan synod, etc. Maybe there is a national initiative that you could contribute to or become a member of.

A checklist for the journey

- Talk things through before you start the curacy, raise important questions about things that really matter. Don't *necessarily* make a big deal about things that you could live with; this may be part of the sacrifice that God may be calling you to make.
- Establish boundaries early on and stick to them as much as possible without being inflexible. We've heard of places where family commitments have been relegated to second or third place despite an original agreement.
- Don't neglect your personal spiritual life – it will sustain you in the difficult times. A car with an empty tank can't be driven anywhere. If we are running on empty, we are not only setting a poor example to our parishioners but are also more likely to make unwise decisions.
- Challenge appropriately.
- Be willing to be vulnerable.
- Training incumbents – be willing to learn from your curate and recognize the transferable skills he or she brings to this new learning environment.
- Be loyal to your clergy colleague, show a united front in public – and thrash out your differences in private.
- Don't be afraid to say that it's not working, and find a way to start again.
- You have a parochial role, but be aware of and engage with the wider Church.
- Remember that you are there to be trained; you are a work in progress.

Beyond the checklist

Recently I was driving in thick fog on a mountain road in Arizona. We were over 7,000 feet above sea level, the clouds were very low, I was on the 'wrong' side of the road and it was pouring with rain. I could hardly see more than a few feet in front of me. It was scary! Fortunately the road had two lanes and I could keep the car at a snail's pace. Soon, however, I realized we were making a descent. Visibility improved as the clouds and fog dispersed, and within a couple of miles I was able to drive with my usual confidence again.

What this anecdote illustrates is that some things can't be prepared for by a checklist (and after all, how boring it would be if following a checklist was all there was to it). In so many of the stories we have read, the clearest indication of how God's guiding hand has come when curates have been called to step outside their comfort zone and trust in his provision.

If you are a curate, we hope these stories have reassured you that with God's help you can make it – but you will have to work at it, make compromises, and be prepared to have some rough edges knocked off. Be vulnerable and learn from your mistakes.

And when you yourself are a training incumbent – don't forget what you learned as a curate. Rachel Wilson's summary is apposite: 'Work is what I do but a priest is what I am.' So ... *go for it!*

References and bibliography

Justine Allain-Chapman, *Resilient Pastors* (London: SPCK, 2012).

T. Berry, 'The Social Construction of the Ministry Student', *Interdisciplinary Journal of Pastoral Studies*, 114 (2004), pp. 23–30.

Neil Burgess, *Into Deep Water* (Bury St Edmunds: Kevin Mayhew, 1998).

George Carey, *The Church in the Marketplace*, 2nd edn (Eastbourne: Kingsway Publications, 1990).

Avery Dulles, *Models of the Church*, 2nd edn (New York: Doubleday, 2000).

The Faith and Order Advisory Group of the Church of England, *The Mission and Ministry of the Whole Church* (London: General Synod, 2007).

Laurie Green, *Let's Do Theology*, 2nd edn (London: Mowbray, 2009).

Mission-Shaped Church: Church Planting and Fresh Expressions of Church in a Changing Context (London: Church House Publishing, 2004).

Lesslie Newbigin, *The Gospel in a Pluralist Society* (Grand Rapids, Mich.: Eerdmans, 1989).

Mike Parsons, *Suicide and the Church: A Pastoral Theology* (Cambridge: Grove Books, 2010).

C. Swift, 'How should Health Care Chaplaincy Negotiate its Professional Identity?', *Interdisciplinary Journal of Pastoral Studies*, 114 (2004), pp. 4–13.

Graham Tomlin, *The Provocative Church*, 3rd edn (London: SPCK, 2008).

Dave Tomlinson, *How to be a Bad Christian . . . and a Better Human Being* (London: Hodder & Stoughton, 2013).

N. T. Wright, *The New Testament and the People of God* (London: SPCK, 1992; reissued 2013).